SEVEN KEYS TO
Spiritual Renewal
WORKBOOK

Seven Keys to

SPIRITUAL

RENEWAL™

Workbook

■

STEPHEN ARTERBURN

and

DAVID STOOP

Edited by Connie Neal

Tyndale House Publishers, Inc.
Wheaton, Illinois

Published in association with the literary agency of Alive Communications, Inc., 1465 Kelly Johnson Blvd., Suite 320, Colorado Springs, CO 80920

Designed by Timothy R. Botts

ISBN 0-8423-6050-6

Printed in the United States of America

04	03	02	01	00	99	98			
10	9	8	7	6	5	4	3	2	1

CONTENTS

INTRODUCTION

THIS WORKBOOK is part of an array of materials we have designed to help you experience spiritual renewal and transformation. Whether you have been searching for God for twenty years or following Christ for twenty years, this material is a guide to growing closer to God and living out his purpose for your life. The *Spiritual Renewal Bible* is part of this collection, and it is available in the New Living Translation and the New International Version. This Bible has notes throughout, devotionals from both Old and New Testaments, character profiles, and book introductions that help you identify and use the seven keys to spiritual renewal. There are also devotionals and profiles that help you to practice various spiritual disciplines. *Seven Keys to Spiritual Renewal* is a book that explains each of the seven keys along with five challenges that commonly interfere with spiritual renewal and transformation. The *Spiritual Renewal Workbook,* which you hold in your hands, gives you a hands-on approach to applying the concepts from the book and the Bible. You may also want to use the *Spiritual Renewal Journal* to record your thoughts and prayers.

The format for this workbook is designed to help you do four things: (1) Understand each key according to its biblical foundation,

(2) learn to use each key, (3) identify where you need to use each key in your life, and (4) remember each key (along with a memory verse and a biblical character who exemplifies using that key).

To accomplish these four goals, we will help you explore the biblical basis for each of the seven keys. You will participate in exercises that cause you to explore, interact with Scripture, and respond directly to God, who alone has the power to grant you spiritual renewal and transformation. While some of the exercises require effort, you will be directed as to where to find the answers in God's Word.

The workbook devotes one week (divided into five days) to each of the seven keys. After the fifth day of the week, you will review the key, the memory verse, and the biblical character who exemplifies using the key. There is also an eighth week devoted to reviewing and applying each of the seven keys once again. At the end of this workbook are samples of some devotionals found in the *Spiritual Renewal Bible*. There is a daily devotional corresponding to each day of the workbook, five for each of the seven keys of spiritual renewal. You may want to supplement your daily work in the workbook with the devotional for that day, or you may want to use these daily devotionals as a follow-up to reinforce what you have learned. Feel free to use them in any way that will help you. Our prayer is that you will not only use these materials but also experience spiritual renewal and transformation as you do.

KEY

ONE

Surrender it!

SEEK GOD

AND

SURRENDER

TO HIM

■

Memory Verses:
Matthew 6:9-10
Pray like this:
Our Father in heaven,
may your name
be honored.
May your Kingdom
come soon.
May your will be done
here on earth,
just as it is in heaven.

KEY ONE
SEEK GOD AND SURRENDER TO HIM

DAY *1*

Are You Seeking God?

■ Read Luke 19:1-10.

The Bible is full of examples of people who sought God and surrendered to him. **Zacchaeus** is one such example. He was a man of wealth, influence, and power. He was respected, feared, and loathed because of his position as a tax collector in Jericho. In those days, tax collectors were notorious for their shady business practices. They often cheated people, collecting more taxes than owed and pocketing the difference. He was regarded as a traitor and an apostate because of his frequent contact with pagans and his willingness to be used as a tool for the Roman oppressors of Israel.

Why would a man like this be driven to climb up a tree to watch a religious teacher walk by? Curiosity? Perhaps. More likely he was driven by a deep spiritual hunger. It's the kind of hunger that comes when one is faced with the emptiness of life apart from God. Although he was rich, Zacchaeus could not buy happiness or satisfaction. The emptiness and longing of his soul caused him to seek God through Jesus.

Surely, Zacchaeus expected to be rejected by Jesus, or at best, ignored. After all, he was a notorious sinner, so he dared not call out to Jesus. But Jesus found him and called out his name. "'Zacchaeus!' he said. 'Quick, come down! For I must be a guest in your home today'" (Luke 19:5). So Zacchaeus came down and welcomed Jesus into his home and his heart.

Something happened to Zacchaeus that day. He was seeking . . . God only knows what. But he looked to Jesus in hopes of finding whatever it was. He dared not tell anyone what he was seeking. He may not have even known himself. But when he turned his heart toward Jesus, Jesus came seeking him. That day Zacchaeus was changed; he became a new man. This was evident by his radical change of heart that caused him to offer to pay back those he had cheated and give half his wealth to the poor. When Jesus saw and heard this, he responded, "Salvation has come to this home today" (Luke 19:9).

Where and to whom did Zacchaeus look when he was seeking?

_____

Where and to whom have you looked in your times of seeking something more out of life?

_____

_____

What did Zacchaeus do that caused Jesus to proclaim, "Salvation has come to this home today"?

_____

_____

If you are a Christian, do you think those watching you would be able to tell that you are by your actions? Is that how they would describe you? If you have surrendered your life to Christ, how has that affected you in such a way that demonstrates that "salvation has come to this home"?

_____

_____

_____

What Are You Seeking?

You have picked up this book because you are seeking something. What is it? Consider the following list, and check any answers that come close to describing your spiritual condition today:

___ You are a Christian and are seeking a deeper relationship with God.

___ You seem to "have it made" in the world (like Zacchaeus), but you're not satisfied.

___ You are not a Christian, but you are hungry for spiritual satisfaction.

___ You've been a Christian a long time but feel distant from God.

___ You're in a crisis and have come to the end of yourself, desiring a new start.

___ You've been turned off by organized religion, but you're spiritually hungry.

___ Other: _____

To What Degree Are You Seeking God?

Jeremiah 29:13-14 reads, "'You will seek me and find me when you seek me with all your heart. I will be found by you,' declares the Lord" (NIV). The promise of finding God is not given to those who seek God casually but to those who do so wholeheartedly.

■ Use the drawing of a heart below, and shade in a representation of how much of your heart is devoted to seeking God right now. If you are halfhearted about your search, shade in half. If you are merely curious, shade in a slight amount. If you are seeking God with your whole heart, shade in the whole heart.

Zacchaeus was wholehearted about seeking and surrendering to God, and he demonstrated this in several ways: He sought out Jesus, climbed a tree to see him, welcomed him publicly, confessed his sin, offered restitution, and became extremely generous.

How do you demonstrate your willingness to seek God and surrender to him?

_____

_____

_____

Does your demonstration of seeking God and surrendering to him match the amount of devotion to him that you indicated by shading in the heart above? If it doesn't match, what does this tell you?

_____

_____

_____

Spiritual Renewal Begins with Jesus Christ

True spiritual renewal cannot begin until you come into a personal relationship with Jesus Christ. The rest of the workbook will not make much sense to you unless you have decided to follow Christ, because only then does he give us the Holy Spirit. The Holy Spirit lives in us and points us to Christ by opening our eyes to understand God's truth. The Bible tells us that "people who aren't Christians can't understand these truths from God's Spirit. It all sounds foolish to them because only those who have the Spirit can understand what the Spirit means" (1 Corinthians 2:14).

Every person belongs to one of two general categories: those who have surrendered—and who must continue to surrender every day—to Christ, or those who are seeking but have not yet surrendered to Jesus Christ. If you are among those who have not yet surrendered to Christ, you also fall under one of two subcategories: either you are convinced that Jesus is the Christ (the one sent from God to save us) and have not yet chosen to surrender to him, or you are not yet convinced and will continue seeking God until you find him. Wherever you are, your journey toward spiritual renewal begins by seeking God and being willing to surrender to him when he reveals himself to you. The following prayers can help you do that.

- If you desire spiritual renewal but have not entered into a personal relationship with Jesus Christ and are still not sure you are ready to surrender to him, here is a suggested prayer for you to pray:

> *Dear God,*
> *I know that there has to be more to life. I am seeking something, and I'm not even sure what it is. I don't know for sure who you are or what you can do in my life, but I come seeking you. Please reveal yourself to me. Please show me the truth about who you are and what you desire to do in my life. Please open my eyes and my heart to see and understand this truth. Please lead me to surrender to you so that I can experience spiritual renewal and transformation. Amen.*

- If you are willing to surrender your life to Jesus Christ, you can pray the following prayer. You will also want to speak to someone in your church or study group who can lead you through God's Word to see the plan of salvation in fuller detail.

> *Dear Jesus,*
> *I know that I have sinned and fallen short of God's ideal for my life. I have hurt myself and others by my wrongdoing. I trust that you died on the cross to pay for all my sins and then rose from the dead, proving that God the Father has accepted your payment on my behalf. I receive you as my Savior. I submit my life to you as my Lord and Master. Please forgive me for all my sins, and cleanse me from every wrong. Please show me how to turn my life around, and empower me to change by your Holy Spirit. Lead me, and I will follow you. Help me to understand and obey your Word, the Bible. Thank you for saving me and granting me eternal life. I pray in your name, Lord Jesus. Amen!*

■ If you are already a Christian but still seek spiritual renewal, you
  can pray the following prayer:

> *Dear Lord Jesus,*
> *I have surrendered my life to you, but I am still seeking more. Show*
> *me specific areas of my life that need to be surrendered to you once*
> *again. Help me today to seek you with my whole heart so that you*
> *may reveal yourself to me and I may find you. Lead me to experience*
> *spiritual renewal and transformation through your Holy Spirit.*
> *Amen!*

How would you describe yourself today as you begin this workbook? Check one of the following:

   ___ I am a seeker who is willing to consider the claims of Jesus
        Christ and seek him, but I am not yet ready to surrender
        the rule of my life over to him.

   ___ I am someone who has just prayed to surrender my life to
        Jesus Christ for the first time.

   ___ I surrendered my life to Jesus Christ on _____ ____,
        _____ (month, day, year).

KEY ONE
SEEK GOD AND
SURRENDER TO HIM

DAY 2

To Whom Are You Surrendering?

When you determine to seek God and sur-
render to him, you need to become familiar with who he is. What is
God's nature and character? What can you expect from him? What
does he think of you? And ultimately, where do you stand in relationship to him? Finding answers to these questions is essential for

spiritual renewal and transformation. Today you will explore what the Bible says about God and how he sees you.

Who is this God to whom you are called to surrender? Ask Job. The Bible says that Job was a righteous man who ended up in the middle of a dispute between the Lord and Satan. Job was very blessed by God, and Satan saw this as the reason for Job's devotion. Satan said that Job would curse God if the blessings were removed, so Job was put to the test. When the unexpected plagues and calamities came one after another, Job sought answers from God, but God remained silent. Eventually God did speak to Job—but not to answer his questions. Instead, God posed some powerful questions of his own. These questions forced Job to recognize the awesome greatness of God and humanity's status before him.

■ Read Job chapters 38–40.

How do these questions change your perception of God, who can answer them all?

_____

_____

_____

The God to whom we are called to surrender is Creator of all that is. He is great, all-powerful, eternal, all-knowing, and wise beyond human understanding. Throughout the Bible we see that any time humans caught some glimpse or revelation of God, either by hearing his voice or by being in his glorious presence, they responded similarly. They would fall facedown before him.

■ Reread Job 40:3-5 to review Job's first response to God's questions. Write out these two verses here:

_____

_____

_____

_____

■ Read Job 42:1-6. Underline what Job learned about God. Circle what Job learned about himself. Below, write what Job decided to do as a result of learning more about God's nature and power (see verse 6):

_____

_____

■ Read Job 42:10-17. Describe the final result of Job's surrender to God:

_____

_____

_____

While we cannot count on material or earthly blessings to follow as a result of surrendering to God, we can be certain that God will bless us. What are some ways in which God may choose to bless us as we surrender to him?

_____

_____

_____

Dare You Trust Such a God?

At both the beginning and the end of his time of suffering, Job demonstrated great faith in the goodness of God and continued to surrender his life to him (see Job 1:21-22; 2:10; 40:4-5; 42:1-6). Do you dare entrust your life to such a God—the God of the Bible? Do you dare surrender to a God who allows pain and suffering? To a God who does not guarantee unabated happiness? To a God who demands our loyalty to him above all else? To a God whose ways are above reproach and beyond our full understanding?

■ Following is a list of some common fears people express about surrendering their lives to God. Check any that apply to you, and give a brief explanation in the line following it:

___ I fear what God might make me do if I surrender to him.

_____

___ I fear the loss of my individuality.

_____

___ I fear that if I surrender my life to God, he won't do what I want him to do.

_____

___ I fear poverty or the loss of material possessions.

_____

___ I fear rejection from those who do not follow God's ways.

_____

___ I fear giving up particular sins that I am not yet willing to give up.

_____

___ I fear that God will punish me.

_____

___ I fear that God will not let me have what I truly desire.

_____

What other apprehensions or fears do you have about surrendering your life to God?

_____

_____

_____

_____

What continues to draw you toward God despite these apprehensions and fears?

_____

_____

_____

You Don't Need to Be Afraid

First John 4:18 is quoted below from the New Living Translation (NLT) of the Bible. One word is repeated in each of the blank spaces below. Even if you are using a different translation, you should be able to determine this word and fill it in each of the blanks.

> *Such love has no _____ because perfect love expels all _____.*
> *If we are afraid, it is for _____ of judgment, and this shows that*
> *his love has not been perfected in us. (1 John 4:18)*

Consider almighty God, whose power and presence are overwhelming to mere mortals. He is Creator of all that is, Commander in Chief of all the forces of heaven, judge of all creation. Anyone who does not tremble at the thought of such an awesome God does not yet know him as he truly is. But what if such a God was willing to be your protector? How would that transform your fear?

_____

_____

_____

■ God always remains the same in nature and power. You, however, can change the way you relate to him by choosing to surrender to him. Look up the verses below and write out the various roles God can play in your life.

Isaiah 54:5 _____

Psalm 91:2 _____

Psalm 12:5 _____

Hebrews 13:6 _____

Romans 8:15 _____

Psalm 23:1 _____

2 Corinthians 1:3-4 _____

1 John 4:8 _____

- Circle any of the titles above that describe how you have known God already.

- Read 1 John 4:8-10 and answer the following questions:

Who is love? _____

How did God show how much he loved us?

_____

If real love is *not* our love for God, what is it?

_____

_____

When you surrender your life to God, you will find confidence in him, for he helps you. Trusting in God allows you to release your fears and know that he cares for you, regardless of what others may do or say.

- Read Hebrews 13:5-6.

What can you say with confidence because God will never fail you or forsake you? The Lord is my _____, so I will not be

_____.

This verse ends with a rhetorical question for you to ponder. If the Lord is your helper, what can mere mortals do to you?

_____

- Memorize Hebrews 13:5-6. Quote these verses to yourself whenever you feel afraid.

KEY ONE
SEEK GOD AND
SURRENDER TO HIM

DAY *3*

What Does It Mean to Surrender?

The concept of surrender can be understood in military terms. *Webster's* dictionary defines surrender as: "the action of yielding one's person or giving up the possession of something especially into the power of another." Try to envision the kingdom of God as a military force over which God is king. Then envision your life as territory over which you rule according to your own moral code and desires. Whenever the forces of two opposing kingdoms collide, one king must eventually surrender to the other or be destroyed. God surrenders to the rule of no human being. Therefore, you must surrender to God or face the consequences.

If you choose to surrender, you give up being the ruler of your own life. You accept peace on his terms and acknowledge God as the ruler of your life. His kingdom operates under his authority and commands, and one of his requirements is that you be righteous, or right before him. But your righteousness does not come by keeping all the commandments or obeying all the laws in the Bible. The righteousness God requires to enter his kingdom can only come by trusting in Jesus Christ to rescue you from your sins. He has taken away the punishment for your sins by dying on the cross for you and rising from the dead. When you surrender to God, he clothes you with Christ's righteousness.

Therefore surrender involves giving up rule over your own life, including trying to be righteous by your own good deeds or sinning as you please. When you surrender to God and submit yourself to his righteous rule, you will still want to do things your way, but you will make the conscious choice to submit to God's will rather than your own. When you surrender your will to God, you recognize his rightful authority and yield to his will. You resign as the ruler of your life and accept the claim God has on your life. You cease to resist him. Surrendering to God does not mean that you suddenly have the power in yourself to keep his commands. Rather, you simply acknowledge that you desire to follow God's will, and he himself will give you the power to do this.

Before you surrender to God, your motto might be: "I can do whatever I want to do." But those who have surrendered to God can take Jesus' words as their motto: "I want your will, not mine" (Matthew 26:39).

Which motto comes closest to describing how your life is ruled?

_____

Being in God's kingdom does not mean that you obey God perfectly and continually. But it does mean that his standards and commands form the basis for your determination of right and wrong. You acknowledge that God's rules are the ones by which you evaluate your life. Whenever you step outside God's moral boundaries, you will recognize that as sin, confess it as such, and receive the forgiveness afforded all those who belong to God's kingdom.

■ Read Matthew 6:33, and write it out here:

_____

_____

_____

Some people seek salvation without wanting to surrender to God as king. They want God to give them eternal life, but they don't want to enlist under his command or submit to his authority as the rightful ruler of their life. How is your life demonstrating that you have surrendered yourself to God *and* are seeking to live for him?

_____

_____

_____

Cite a specific example from this past week when you chose to do God's will instead of your will:

_____

_____

Just as obedience to those in authority is the hallmark of a good soldier, obedience to God demonstrates that you have surrendered your life to his righteous rule. One of the words for obedience used in the New Testament is *hupakouo*. It is made up of two root words, *hupo* ("under") and *akouo* ("hear"). The word connotes the idea of hearing what has been said and placing yourself under it. You are called to obey God. When you do, you give evidence that you have heard God's Word, believed it, and now are placing yourself under its demands.

■ Read James 1:22-23 and 4:17.

What is one thing God's Word has prompted you to do or to change in your life?

_____

_____

Surrender Is Seldom Once-and-for-All or All at Once

You may be thinking, "Well, I'm a Christian. I handled this surrender business when I accepted Christ." While there is an important moment when you choose to "give your life to Christ," you must also continually bring yourself under the righteous rule of God. In this regard, the Christian life is like a marriage. When you get married, you surrender your entire future to be in union with your spouse. But on a day-to-day basis, one must continually yield to the other; you must remind yourself of your commitment and choose daily to surrender your "right" to demand your own way.

What areas of your life present the greatest challenge in terms of continually surrendering your will to God each day?

_____

God wants your entire life surrendered to his righteous rule. Consider each of the following areas of life, and indicate how well you continually surrender it to God's rule. "1" indicates that you have not surrendered this area at all, and "5" indicates complete surrender.

Poor/Good

1 2 3 4 5 Your reputation and public image

1 2 3 4 5 Your moral conduct

1 2 3 4 5 Your thoughts and fantasies

1 2 3 4 5 Your personal life and actions that others never see

1 2 3 4 5 Your career

1 2 3 4 5 Your commitments to other people

1 2 3 4 5 Your relationships (family, church, community, work, friendships)

1 2 3 4 5 Your emotions (fear, worry, anger, sorrow, etc.)

1 2 3 4 5 Your finances and material possessions

1 2 3 4 5 Your future

1 2 3 4 5 Your pride

Since obedience involves (1) hearing what God says and (2) submitting to God's commands, you can't surrender an area of your life in obedience to God unless you know what God's Word says regarding it. Circle the items you marked with a low score and explore God's Word to see how he calls you to live in that regard. Use a concordance or discuss the issue with a more mature Christian to find Bible verses that address that particular area of life. Then begin to surrender this area to God's will each day.

This exercise may be difficult because you may realize how much of your life is not yet under God's righteous rule. If you are disappointed with how you are doing, don't get discouraged. The fact that you are seeking God regarding your whole life is good. Remember, the Holy Spirit is at work in you. He will guide you as you surrender your life to God. He will also give you the power you need to change. God doesn't tell you to clean up your act. He tells you to surrender, as you are, to him. Then the Holy Spirit can begin the process of transforming you.

It is only by the power of the Holy Spirit that you can live as God intends. Godly behavior comes from a continual process of your remaining in and yielding to Jesus, just as a branch draws nourishment from the vine that it remains connected to (John 15:5). As you continually surrender to God, your life will bear the fruit of the Holy Spirit: love, joy, peace, patience, kindness, goodness, faithfulness, gentleness, and self-control (Galatians 5:22-23).

KEY ONE
SEEK GOD AND
SURRENDER TO HIM

DAY 4

Let Go and Let God

Surrendering ourselves to God involves letting go of control and allowing God to be God—not just God of the universe but God of your life. Some people "follow" God because they want to use him to do their own will. But true surrender means letting go of your demands and allowing God to shape your life according to his design and his will. In other words, God rules us; we don't rule God.

■ Read Jeremiah 18:1-6.

To what does God liken himself in this passage?

_____

To what does God liken his people in this passage?

_____

How much control does the clay have over what the potter does with it?

_____

- Read Isaiah 45:9.

What lesson are God's people to draw from the clay in the potter's hands? The clay does not _____ with its maker. It does not say,

_____

_____

Are you willing to allow God to shape your life as he sees fit? How will you demonstrate your willingness to let go and let God shape your life?

_____

_____

_____

- Read Romans 6:19-23.

According to this passage, we are either slaves to sin or slaves to righteousness. Paul notes the benefits to those who surrender their bodies to righteousness.

When you yield your body to righteousness it leads to _____, and the result is _____ _____.

When you yield to sin, it results in _____.

The Best Example of Surrender

Jesus is our perfect example of surrender to God. He surrendered to the will of his Father throughout his earthly ministry. He told his disciples, "I will do what the Father requires of me, so that the world will know that I love the Father" (John 14:31).

Sometimes surrendering to the Father's will required difficult tasks of Jesus. This is clearly seen in the garden of Gethsemane, where the path of surrender led Jesus to his knees. He knew that the cross awaited him, yet his prayer reflects perfect submission to his Father's plan.

■ Read Mark 14:32-36.

Do you think Jesus found it easy to surrender his will to God? What makes you think this?

_____

_____

_____

What did Jesus want his Father to do if it was possible?

_____

_____

What did Jesus pray that showed his willingness to surrender to his Father's will?

_____

_____

If Jesus Christ himself was in anguish as he surrendered his will to do the Father's will, do you expect that your surrender to God will always be easy? _____

Surrender Comes in the Form of a Cross

■ Read Matthew 16:24-25; Mark 8:34-35; and Luke 9:23-24.

What three things does Jesus Christ call us to do if we are to surrender to him?

_____

_____

_____

Luke's Gospel added one detail. How often did Luke say the followers of Jesus must shoulder their cross?

_____

How can you put aside your selfish ambition *today* in order to obey the will of your Father in heaven?

_____

_____

Hebrews 12:2 tells us that Jesus was willing to surrender to the Father's will and go to the cross "because of the joy he knew would be his afterward." What gives you hope and motivation as you strive to surrender to God's will?

KEY ONE
SEEK GOD AND SURRENDER TO HIM

 DAY 5

Surrender Must Be Unconditional

Often when people are in need of something, they try to bargain with God to get it. They promise to serve God all of their days *if* he will do thus and such for them. That is manipulation, not surrender. God is not in the business of making deals to get you to do what he wants you to do. He demands that we come to him humbly, giving up our selfish ambition and desires.

What kinds of bargains have you tried to strike with God?

_____

_____

_____

Trying to manipulate God like this is not true surrender to him. Spend a moment reflecting upon these bargains, and ask God to help you submit to him unconditionally. The following prayer can help direct your thoughts in this way.

> *Father in heaven,*
> *I am sorry that I have tried to manipulate you in the past by*
>
> _____.
>
> *I put conditions on our relationship instead of simply trusting you and surrendering my life to your righteous rule. Please forgive me for making my attitude toward you conditional.*
> *Thank you for sending Jesus to die for my sins so that you could offer me unconditional love and acceptance. I trust you enough to surrender my life to you without condition or demands. I trust you to love me, to take care of me, and to never leave me. Please help me to realize whenever I am trying to control you, so that I can surrender to you and let you control my life. Amen.*

Surrender Calls for Contentment

Another component of true surrender involves being content with what God has given us.

■ Read Philippians 4:11-13.

What was the apostle Paul's secret to being content?

_____

_____

Does this passage indicate that God's people will always have plenty? _____

Does it indicate that God's people will always have little? _____

Paul had learned to get along happily, whether he had plenty or whether he was in need. What was the secret to his happiness?

_____

_____

When have you known what it's like to have plenty?

_____

_____

When have you known what it's like to be in need?

_____

_____

Christ is the secret to getting along happily in both situations.

List some things you have complained about in the last week:

1. _____

2. _____

3. _____

Of all the things you have complained about, which ones have you specifically brought before God in prayer? _____

- Take each item you have not prayed for and pray about it now, asking God to help you through it or to change the situation.

- Read 1 Timothy 6:6-8.

What is Paul's rationale for why we should be content with what we have?

_____

_____

According to these verses, what two things should be enough to make us content?

_____

_____

What does it take to make you happy? List several things that you must learn to be content without:

_____

_____

_____

■ As you read the passage below, underline the troubles that await those who are not content. Then circle everything Paul told Timothy to pursue.

> But people who long to be rich fall into temptation and are trapped by many foolish and harmful desires that plunge them into ruin and destruction. For the love of money is at the root of all kinds of evil. And some people, craving money, have wandered from the faith and pierced themselves with many sorrows. But you, Timothy, belong to God; so run from all these evil things, and follow what is right and good. Pursue a godly life, along with faith, love, perseverance, and gentleness. (1 Timothy 6:9-11)

Part of being completely surrendered to God involves pursuing the things of God. For each of the items listed in Paul's letter to Timothy, consider how you will pursue this in your own life.

How will you pursue . . .

a godly life? _____

_____

faith? _____

_____

love? _____

_____

24

perseverance? _____

_____

gentleness? _____

_____

A good test to see if we are surrendering ourselves to God and learn-ing to be content is how we handle our finances. In both Matthew 6:24 and Luke 16:13, Jesus tells his followers, "No one can serve two mas-ters. For you will hate one and love the other, or be devoted to one and despise the other. You cannot serve both God and money." How do your finances reflect your surrender (or lack of surrender) to God?

_____

_____

When you face a decision, which factor tends to carry the most weight for you, the financial impact or the spiritual impact?

Reviewing Key 1
What is the first key to spiritual renewal?

_____

The biblical character who exemplifies this key for us is Zacchaeus. In your own words, describe how Zacchaeus exemplified seeking God and surrendering to him:

_____

_____

_____

_____

_____

Write out your memory verses from Matthew 6:9-10 here:

_____

_____

_____

_____

In what ways have you begun to seek God and surrender to him?

_____

_____

_____

What areas of your life still need to be surrendered to God?

_____

_____

_____

TWO

See it!

SEE

THE

TRUTH

■

Memory Verses:
Psalm 139:23-24
Search me, O God,
and know my heart;
test me and know
my thoughts.
Point out anything in
me that offends you,
and lead me along the
path of everlasting life.

KEY TWO
SEE THE TRUTH

DAY *1*

A Man after God's Own Heart

The memory verses for this week were penned by **David,** our biblical example of someone who could see the truth—the second key to spiritual renewal. By God's blessing, David killed a giant, soothed a raging king, led his armies to victory, and became the greatest king in Israel's history. From his earliest days, David loved and worshiped God. He longed to be close to God and laid his life before his Creator. David often welcomed God's examination of his life, and many times he wholeheartedly accepted God's correction. In these times, David demonstrated that he was a man who came to God with eyes wide open, willing and able to see the truth about God and himself.

Other times, however, David was not so quick to see the truth about his life. Sometimes he seemed to ignore the truth that was right before his eyes, especially when that truth revealed his own sinfulness. Yet David was still called a man after God's own heart (1 Samuel 13:14). This should give us hope that we, too, can still please God, though we often fail to see the truth about God and ourselves.

■ Read Acts 13:22 and fill in the blanks in this quote of what God said of David: "David son of Jesse is a man after ____ _____ _____, for he will do _____ I want him to."

Even though God approved of David and held him up as an example, the Bible tells us of several stages of David's life when he didn't see the truth so clearly.

■ Read the following Bible passages and write the reference next to the matching description of David's spiritual condition and willingness to see the truth:

2 Samuel 12:13
2 Samuel 11:1-5
Psalm 51
2 Samuel 11:6-21
2 Samuel 12:7-12
Psalm 26
2 Samuel 12:1-6

_____ David was a young man, desiring to see the truth and be fully assured that he was right with God.

_____ David was seeing something other than God's will. He lusted and disregarded God's commands.

_____ David was blinded by his own sin. He tried to hide the wrong he had done so no one else would see it.

_____ God's prophet came to David and presented a story that described the sin David had committed. But David was blind to his own sin, and he condemned himself with his answer.

_____ David's eyes were opened when a prophet revealed God's knowledge of his sin and the punishment he would bear.

_____ David finally saw the truth and admitted his sin.

_____ This is David's prayer of confession and repentance and a plea for God to restore the joy of his salvation.

■ Think of specific times when your spiritual vision was similar to David's regarding sin.

Describe a time when you allowed something sinful to cause you to disregard God's commands:

_____

_____

_____

Describe a time when you ignored the truth of your sin and tried to hide your sin from others as well:

_____

_____

_____

How did trying to hide the truth affect your relationship with God?

_____

_____

Describe a time when you hypocritically condemned someone else for a sin that you yourself were guilty of and were blinded to at the time:

_____

_____

_____

Describe a time when someone confronted you about your sin and its consequences, causing you to see that God knew what you had done:

_____

_____

How did seeing the truth make you feel? What did you do? What should you have done?

_____

_____

_____

Search Me, O God!

■ Pray aloud the following (a prayer taken from the words of David in Psalm 139:1-7, 11-12, 23-24): "O Lord, you have examined my heart and know everything about me. You know when I sit down or stand up. You know my every thought when far away. You chart the path ahead of me and tell me where to stop and rest. Every moment you know where I am. You know what I am going to say even before I say it, Lord. You both precede and follow me. You place your hand of blessing on my head. Such knowledge is too wonderful for me, too great for me to know! I can never escape from your spirit! I can never get away from your presence! . . . I could ask the darkness to hide me and the light around me to become night—but even in darkness I cannot hide from you. To you the night shines as bright as day. Darkness and light are both alike to you. . . . Search me, O God, and know my heart; test me and know my thoughts. Point out anything in me that offends you, and lead me along the path of everlasting life. Amen."

KEY TWO
SEE THE TRUTH

DAY 2

Living in the Light

If you want to see the truth spiritually, you must stop living in spiritual darkness and live in spiritual light. Colossians 1:12-13 tells of two kingdoms: Satan's kingdom and Christ's kingdom.

What is Satan's kingdom characterized by? _____

What is Christ's kingdom characterized by? _____

Ephesians 5:8 is addressed to Christians. If you are a Christian, what does it say you once were filled with? _____
What does it say you are filled with now? _____

How is this change in our hearts reflected in our lives?

_____

_____

Even though God's people are called to live in the light (1 John 1:7) and see the truth, sometimes we allow our spiritual vision to be impaired. The consequences for failing to recognize and correct this problem are serious. The Bible describes several ways in which our spiritual vision can be impaired, causing us to ignore the truth. As you read, also consider the consequences of each problem if it is left unchecked.

1. Focusing on the faults and shortcomings of others while remaining oblivious to our own.

■ Read Matthew 7:1-5.

This passage rebukes those who detail what is wrong with others while they themselves possess the same faults. Though they think they are so insightful regarding other people's sins, actually they are blinded by their own sins, which they are not even aware of. People with this problem are often called self-righteous.

2. Hiding sin that we have committed instead of confessing it and repenting.

■ Read 2 Samuel 11–12.

The events surrounding David's adultery with Bathsheba show another way we can allow our spiritual sight to become clouded.

33

David knew that he had sinned, but he chose to ignore his conscience and tried to cover up his sin. It was only after the prophet Nathan led him to see his own guilt that he confessed his sin and repented. Like David, you may have hidden something from the light of truth, and your ability to see your guilt has been impaired. It may take someone else to confront you with your sin and cause you to recognize your guilt.

3. Choosing to overlook the sins of those around us because we do not want to deal with them.

■ Read 2 Samuel 13.

David closed his eyes to a sinful situation in his family. David's son Amnon became consumed with lust for his half-sister Tamar, so he devised a scheme and raped her. David found out what had happened and became angry, but apparently he did not take action against Amnon. In effect, he closed his eyes to it. Perhaps he didn't confront his son's sin because it reminded him of his own sin with Bathsheba. The result of David's inaction was that Tamar's full-brother, Absalom, avenged her by killing Amnon. When you choose to ignore obvious problems among those you are responsible for, you are acting like David. You may discover that this happens most often when situations remind you of your own sins and shortcomings.

For each of the three forms of spiritual blindness mentioned above, think of an occasion in your own life when you have acted in such a way:

1. _____

_____

_____

2. _____

_____

_____

3. _____

_____

Choosing to ignore the truth may allow us to avoid something unpleasant or difficult for a time, but living in darkness like this is always dangerous. You need to be able to see the light of truth and walk in it. In order to do this, you must maintain your spiritual eyesight. If you need to have your spiritual eyesight corrected, you may want to pray the prayer below or compose one of your own.

> *Lord, please give me eyes that see the truth. I ask you to send your light into my life, so that I can see where I have fallen short of your perfect standards. As I walk in the light, I trust you to cleanse me from all my sins through the blood of your Son. Amen.*

■ Read 1 John 2:9-10.

In Luke 11:34-36, Jesus tells his followers: "Your eye is a lamp for your body. A pure eye lets sunshine into your soul. But an evil eye shuts out the light and plunges you into darkness. Make sure that the light you think you have is not really darkness. If you are filled with light, with no dark corners, then your whole life will be radiant, as though a floodlight is shining on you."

■ Reflect on these questions and answer them to yourself:

Are there any areas of your life where you do not want the light of truth to shine?

Are there "dark corners" in your life—places where you hide sins that you do not want to deal with and that you do not want others to know about?

Can you call your life radiant?

1 John 1:7 notes two things that accompany living in the light of God's presence. What are they?

35

1. _____

2. _____

Let the light of God's presence into your life and experience these blessings he has assured us of.

KEY TWO
SEE THE TRUTH

DAY 3

Why Do We Avoid Seeing the Truth?

Even though seeing the truth is a key to spiritual renewal, the truth can be scary. Sometimes the harsh reality of the truth and the difficult consequences of facing it seem reason enough to continue in a "see no evil" mode.

■ Consider the following reasons why someone would avoid the truth, and mark any that you can identify with. Circle "Now" if it is a reason you are currently using to avoid some truth about yourself and "Past" if it is a reason you have used before. After each reason marked, past or present, write a description of the truth you were trying to avoid.

1. You avoid the truth because you have grown used to living in the dark. The prospect of light shining on the situation makes you afraid of how life might change and the pain that might come.

Now/Past Description of the truth I was (or am) trying to avoid:

_____

_____

2. You avoid the truth because it may bring negative consequences. Seeing the truth often comes with a price, and you may lose your

career, your income, your family, your possessions, your friends, or your reputation. It might disrupt your marriage or other important relationships.

Now/Past Description of the truth I was (or am) trying to avoid:

_____

_____

3. You may avoid seeing the truth because of pride. Our culture says, "Do it your way!" If you buy into that motto, your ego can stand in the way of seeing the truth, especially if the truth reveals that your way isn't working or that you need help.

Now/Past Description of the truth I was (or am) trying to avoid:

_____

_____

4. You may avoid seeing the truth because you don't want to give up control over some area of your life.

Now/Past Description of the truth I was (or am) trying to avoid:

_____

_____

5. The most common reason you may avoid seeing the truth is that you already know deep down that you have done something wrong but you are not ready to confess it, accept responsibility for your actions, and repent. You may even be trying to maintain some semblance of a good relationship with God without having to deal with your sin.

Now/Past Description of the truth I was (or am) trying to avoid:

_____

_____

■ Ultimately, all these reasons are grounded in one single problem. This problem is revealed in John 3:19-20. Write out these verses of Scripture here:

_____

_____

_____

_____

_____

■ Write out 1 John 1:5-6 here:

_____

_____

_____

_____

_____

Some Ways People Avoid Seeing the Truth
Just as people may have various *reasons* for avoiding the truth, they may also have various *ways* of avoiding the truth.

■ Consider the list below and mark each statement that describes something you tend to do. Again, if this is something you do now, circle "Now," and if it is something you have done at some time in the past, circle "Past." While this behavior doesn't prove that you are avoiding seeing the truth or accepting reality, it may be a clue to something you cannot see clearly. After you complete the list honestly, pray and ask the Lord to reveal to you if any of these behaviors are serving to keep you from seeing the truth.

1. You keep busy—possibly even with good things—so you don't have to think about issues you want to avoid. Now/Past
2. You avoid prayer. Now/Past
3. You avoid times of silence and introspection. Now/Past

4. You avoid honest conversations that touch anywhere near a sensitive area of your life. Now/Past

5. You minimize or rationalize behavior that is sinful to God. Now/Past

6. You avoid people whom you associate with spiritual matters or who seem to be living a life that pleases God. Now/Past

James 1:22-25 describes God's Word as being like a mirror. When you look into it, you should see the truth about yourself. If you look intently at yourself and reflect on your life in the light of God's Word, you can be transformed. But you must see the truth as God sees it. It is only as you see the truth about your sin that you can confess it and be cleansed from it. Then you can begin to walk in the light, just as Christ is in the light, and you will experience fellowship with other believers and the joy of being forgiven from your sins. Therefore, whenever you allow any part of your life to remain in the dark, you hinder God's process of transformation in your life.

■ Read Hebrews 4:13 aloud to yourself. Ask God to reveal any sin in your life that you may not see. Then spend fifteen minutes in silence, meditating on the truth of this verse and anything the Holy Spirit brings to your mind.

KEY TWO
SEE THE TRUTH

DAY **4**

God Reveals Our Sin

When the light of truth shines on sinful human beings, it forces them to stop relying on their own merits, or righteousness. When people see the truth, they stop pretending things aren't "so bad" and come to God with a realistic view of themselves, including both the good and the bad. They begin to seek God's help in the spiritual growth process—a process that continues throughout life.

God's light will reveal your imperfections and sins. This can be quite a blow to human pride. But that is good! Human pride is the source of most sin and separation from God. Therefore, it is only when God's "inner light" provides the illumination we need to see the truth that the possibility of transformation becomes real. You must see yourself as you are—as we all are—flawed, unholy, in need of redemption and complete reformation. Every person must see their need for forgiveness and cleansing, for righteousness and strength to please God. If you delude yourself into thinking you are somehow a "cut above the rest" and never see the truth of your fallen human condition, your soul remains in grave danger, and your chances of true spiritual renewal are miniscule. But when you see yourself as you really are—sinful yet valuable to God, weak yet gifted by God—then spiritual renewal is possible.

God Reveals the Remedy for Sin

The spiritual key of seeing the truth has two facets: seeing the truth of your human condition and seeing the truth of God's provision for your condition. Without seeing the truth of what God has done for us, everyone would be terrified to see the truth. Most people know they would not fare very well under close scrutiny of their lives. But once you realize that God has provided a remedy for sin and offers you freedom from it, your fears will be eliminated. For the Bible tells us that God has provided more than enough grace to deal with all the sin that has been committed (Romans 5:20). So the more you see your sinfulness, the more you appreciate the grace of God.

■ Write out 2 Corinthians 5:21:

_____

_____

_____

Jesus never sinned, but what did God make him?

_____

On whose behalf did he do this? _____

Why did he do this?

_____

Pray that God will show you the beautiful truth of this verse. When you accept the truth that your sin can be removed and that you can be made right with God, you don't have to be afraid to see the truth about yourself. In fact, it is only when the light of truth reveals your sinfulness that you can experience this wonderful reality.

■ Read Romans 1:28-32.

   Whom does this passage describe? _____

   Do you fit into this category? _____

■ Read Romans 2:1-4.

   Whom does this passage describe?

   _____

   Do you fit into this category? _____

■ Read Romans 3:9-12.

   According to this passage, who is righteous in God's eyes?

   _____

So how many people need to see the truth of their own sinfulness and turn to God to receive his forgiveness and have him transform their lives? _____

These words were written by the apostle Paul. Before he became a Christian, Paul was known as Saul, and he spent his entire life learning the teachings of the Pharisees and advancing in status among them. He depended on his Jewish heritage, his religious zeal, and his keeping of the law to make him right with God. Because of this, he hated Christians, who preached a message of grace and forgiveness of sin. Saul went in search of them and persecuted them until, literally, he "saw the light."

■ Read the account of Saul's conversion in Acts 8:1-3 and Acts 9:1-30.

According to Philippians 3:4-6, how did Saul compare to anyone else who put confidence in their own efforts to please God?

_____

Before seeing the grace of God in Jesus Christ, who takes away all our sins, Saul did not dare see the truth about his sinful human nature. He may have been able to measure up to the external requirements of the law, but no one can fully obey the true intent of the law, for it reaches down to the true motives and intentions of our sinful hearts. Jesus showed this in the Sermon on the Mount (see Matthew 5–7).

According to Psalm 51:6, what does God desire?

_____

After Saul became a Christian and changed his name to Paul, he became a leader in the church. In his letter to the Romans, Paul reflected on his inability to keep the law and his struggle with sin. His words give us great insight into our own tendency toward sin and disobedience.

■ Read Romans 7:14-24.

Give an example of how you have experienced the struggle with sin that Paul describes in these verses.

_____

_____

■ Read Romans 7:25–8:2.

Who is the answer to our struggle with sin? _____

Will those who belong to Christ Jesus be condemned for their sin?

_____

What can free us from slavery to sin?

_____

■ Read 1 John 1:8-9. According to these verses, what demonstrates that we are fooling ourselves and refusing to accept the truth?

_____

One reason you may say you have no sin is because you may not see the truth about yourself. And you may be refusing to see the truth about yourself because you fear there is no remedy for your sin. No matter how dark your sin, no matter how powerful its hold on you, Jesus Christ has the power to free you, completely forgive you, and cleanse you from all unrighteousness.

KEY TWO
SEE THE TRUTH

DAY **5**

Getting Help to See the Truth

If someone were to walk up to a blind man and command him to "see the truth," it would do no good unless the blind man were also given the ability to see. He may be willing to see, but he is unable. Part of seeing the truth involves being willing to see; but some aspects of the truth can only be seen if *God* gives you the ability to see them.

■ Read John 16:13.

What does Jesus associate the Spirit with? _____

What does Jesus promise that the Spirit will do when he comes?

_____

If you are a Christian, you have the Spirit to lead you into truth. Think of specific times that God's Spirit has guided you, and then write a prayer of thanks to God:

_____

_____

_____

■ Read 2 Timothy 3:16 and Hebrews 4:12.

As we learned on Day 3, God also uses his Word to show us the truth about ourselves. We can use it much like a ruler against our lives to see how we measure up. We can also be certain that God's Word will cut us to the core, exposing our true hearts so that we can deal with our sins.

Even though you may call upon God's Spirit and read his Word, however, sometimes it is difficult to see the truth by yourself. This is one of the reasons God calls us to be in relationship with other Christians. Mature Christians—especially those who know you well—can help you see the truth about yourself and how God can transform you.

■ Make a list of people you can talk to about spiritual matters. These people should be able to confront you about problems they see in your life and help you to learn how to deal with them.

1._____

2._____

3._____

■ Make it a daily prayer to ask God to open your eyes to the truth about yourself. When he shows you things that need to be changed, ask him to help you.

Reviewing Key 2

What is the second key to spiritual renewal?

_____

The biblical character who exemplifies this key for us is David. In your own words, describe one instance when David *did* use this key and one instance when he did *not:*

Did:_____

_____

_____

Did not: _____

_____

_____

What did you learn from David about becoming blind to the truth:

_____

_____

_____

Write out your memory verses from Psalm 139:23-24 here:

_____

_____

_____

_____

What new truths have you seen about yourself as a result of this week's exercises?

_____

_____

_____

_____

KEY

THREE

Say it!

SPEAK

THE

TRUTH

■

Memory Verse:
James 5:16
*Confess your sins
to each other and
pray for each other
so that you may be healed.
The earnest prayer of a
righteous person has
great power and
wonderful results.*

KEY THREE
SPEAK THE TRUTH

DAY *1*

What Does Speaking the Truth Mean?

Now that you have surrendered yourself to God and seen the truth about yourself and God, the next step is to speak, or confess, the truth. This is our third key to spiritual renewal.

The Greek word for confess, *homologeo*, comes from *homos* ("same") and *lego* ("speak"). These root words give us insight into the fuller meaning of confession, or speaking the truth. It seems to carry the sense of "assent" or "agreement with." When you make a confession, you are coming into agreement with what God says, whether this deals with your life, with God himself, or with anything else. You agree that what God says is right is right, and what he says is wrong is wrong. When you make a personal confession, you are assessing your life as God sees it and admitting where you are wrong.

■ Pray and ask the Holy Spirit to help you see yourself as God sees you. Ask him to reveal anything in your life that needs to be realigned with his desires.

Five Ways to Speak the Truth

Since the definition of confession, "to agree with God," is fairly

49

broad, there are a number of ways in which a person can confess something. Following are five of those ways:

To confess something can mean
1. *To declare a belief*
2. *To admit guilt regarding an accusation*
3. *To openly and freely declare a fault or sin*
4. *To praise*
5. *To promise*

Below we have given you an example of each kind of confession. After each example, practice speaking the truth by "confessing" something from your own life or experience that fits the example.

1. *To declare a belief*
Example: Romans 10:9 says, "If you confess with your mouth that Jesus is Lord and believe in your heart that God raised him from the dead, you will be saved." Those who are Christians confess the beliefs mentioned in this verse.

Your example:

_____

_____

_____

2. *To admit guilt regarding an accusation*
Example: A criminal who pleads guilty to the charges brought against him makes a confession. In a similar way, the Bible tells us that we are all sinful before God (Romans 3:23), a truth which all of us must confess eventually.

Your example:

_____

_____

_____

3. *To openly and freely declare a fault or sin*
Example: Sharing something with a group of believers such as, "I have a problem with my temper," is making a confession.

Your example:

_____

_____

_____

4. *To praise*
Example: Hebrews 13:15 says, "With Jesus' help, let us continually offer our sacrifice of praise to God by proclaiming the glory of his name." The Greek word that is translated "proclaiming the glory" in this verse is *homologeo* ("confess"). We can praise God by confessing his greatness.

Your example:

_____

_____

_____

5. *To promise*
Example: When a couple exchanges wedding vows, they are confessing promises to each other.

Your example:

_____

_____

_____

From these examples you can see that confession, or speaking the truth, is not just admitting guilt, though that is certainly one aspect of it. You can also find encouragement as you speak the truth of God's blessings and promises to his people. For instance, we can rejoice in the confession that "Jesus Christ is the same yesterday, today, and forever" (Hebrews 13:8).

What are some encouraging truths from God's Word that you can confess?

1. _____

_____

2. _____

_____

3. _____

_____

Speaking the Truth Properly

No matter which of the five ways we are speaking the truth, the Bible gives specific guidelines for how we are to speak the truth.

■ Read the following verses:

Romans 9:1
2 Corinthians 4:13
Ephesians 4:15
Ephesians 4:25
Ephesians 5:19
James 1:19

Which verse above is summarized by the following statements?

_____ Speak the truth with a clear conscience.
_____ Speak in keeping with what you truly believe.
_____ Speak truthfully, without lying or falsehood.
_____ Speak to each other in psalms, hymns, and spiritual songs.
_____ Be slow to speak, not speaking rashly in anger.
_____ Speak the truth in love.

There is great power for good in speaking God's truth. Below is a list of ways in which God's spoken truth has effected or is effecting a significant result.

Genesis 1:3	God spoke the world into existence.
Luke 4:4, 8, 12	Jesus quoted Scripture in response to Satan's temptations.
John 1:1, 14	Jesus is the Word of God made flesh.
Romans 10:9	Salvation is contingent on confessing that Jesus is Lord.
Hebrews 13:15	Praise—the fruit of your lips—is an acceptable sacrifice to God.
James 5:16	Confessing sins to each other brings healing.

■ Pray and ask God to show you how you can bring healing and hope to yourself and others by speaking his truths.

KEY THREE
SPEAK THE TRUTH

DAY 2

Obstacles to Confessing Sins

People have a natural tendency to hide or mask their sins, problems, or uncomfortable feelings. Some people have grown up in families that hid embarrassing problems, such as alcohol abuse, adultery, or financial woes, and thus were taught to be secretive. They were taught that to speak the truth was to betray their family. Others have had parents or siblings who used embarrassment for their own purposes, instilling in these people a sense of mistrust early on and a reluctance to reveal personal information to anyone. Still others have had their emotions disrespected or rebuked and may continue to hide them—even if they are in an apparently safe environment. Those who have grown up under constant disapproving scrutiny of their words may have learned that it is best to say nothing at all. Childhood lessons tend to stick with you, whether the lessons were good or bad.

■ Take a personal assessment of what makes you hesitate to speak out or confess the truth openly to God and others. Check any of the following that apply to you:

    ___ I grew up in a family that was secretive.

    ___ In my family, to reveal an embarrassing truth was considered betrayal.

    ___ I learned that my embarrassing secrets could be used as a weapon against me.

    ___ When I spoke, even truthfully, others often disapproved of what I said.

    ___ When I expressed my feelings, they were often disrespected by others.

Along with these aversions to confession that are learned from childhood, there are several other common fears that keep many people from revealing their sins. From the list below, check any fears you experience when you consider confessing your sins to other Christians. Deciding which fears you possess will probably be made easier if you bear in mind a particular issue you have kept secret.

    ___ The fear of showing weakness or being perceived as needing help

    ___ The fear of a damaged reputation

    ___ The fear of others knowing your secrets and being publicly exposed

    ___ The fear of retaliation from those you have hurt

    ___ The fear of rejection

    ___ The fear of having to give up the sin once you confess it

    ___ The fear of admitting responsibility and no longer being seen simply as a victim

    ___ The fear of change once you confess your sin

    ___ The fear of bearing the consequences of your behavior

___ The fear of losing control over a situation

___ Other fears: _____

_____

Remember, the more you keep secrets, the more you isolate yourself from God and others in God's family. There is a spiritual and emotional price to pay for refusing to speak the truth. What negative effects have you seen in your spiritual and emotional life that originate with a refusal to speak the truth as God tells you to do?

_____

_____

_____

Have you ever vowed never to tell a living soul about a certain sin?

_____

If so, why did you make that vow?

_____

_____

_____

How has keeping this secret burdened your soul?

_____

_____

_____

Have you confessed this sin to God?

_____

Who was or is affected by this sin or by your refusal to reveal it?

_____

_____

What might happen if you were to confess the truth about this sin to God and to the appropriate people?

_____

_____

_____

Each person has a different picture that comes to mind when he or she thinks of confession. The Bible's picture of confession, or speaking the truth, is a positive one, even though some of its consequences may be painful. What picture comes to mind for you when you think of confession or speaking the truth?

_____

God doesn't command you to tell everyone everything about your life, but you should be able to share the truth about your life with someone. If fear prevents you from doing so, it needs to be counteracted by faith in God, who promises to forgive, protect, deliver, and restore. Since God has required confession, you can trust that when you obey him, he will uphold you with his presence, provision, and grace.

■ Start to speak the truth by confessing how you feel about being open and honest. Compose a letter to God. Include the following parts: (1) Tell him about any hesitations or fears you have about confessing your sins to him or to others; (2) tell him any secrets that you have vowed never to tell anyone, along with what you think may happen if you divulged your secrets to anyone; (3) ask God to give you wisdom to know what needs to be confessed to another person; (4) ask God to guide you to someone with whom you can safely share the truth about yourself.

You may want to compose the letter on a separate sheet of paper so that you can keep it in a private place if you wish. Or you can compose it here:

_____

_____

_____

_____

_____

_____

_____

KEY THREE
SPEAK THE TRUTH

DAY*3*

A Portrait of Confession

Refusing to confess sin to God or to another person always has damaging consequences. **King David** wrote from personal experience when he wrote Psalm 32, which is printed below.

■ Read the psalm and then do the following: Underline sentences that describe the effects of keeping sin secret or refusing to confess sin. Circle sentences that detail the benefits of confession. Put a box around what God did as a result of David's confession.

> ¹*Oh, what joy for those*
> *whose rebellion is forgiven,*
> *whose sin is put out of sight!*
> ²*Yes, what joy for those*
> *whose record the* LORD *has cleared of sin,*
> *whose lives are lived in complete honesty!*
>
> ³*When I refused to confess my sin,*
> *I was weak and miserable,*
> *and I groaned all day long.*
> ⁴*Day and night your hand of discipline was heavy on me.*

My strength evaporated like water in the summer heat.
Interlude

[5]*Finally, I confessed all my sins to you*
and stopped trying to hide them.
I said to myself, "I will confess my rebellion to the LORD."
And you forgave me! All my guilt is gone.
Interlude

[6]*Therefore, let all the godly confess their rebellion to you while there*
is time,
that they may not drown in the floodwaters of judgment.
[7]*For you are my hiding place;*
you protect me from trouble.
You surround me with songs of victory.
Interlude

[8]*The LORD says, "I will guide you along the best pathway for your life.*
I will advise you and watch over you.
[9]*Do not be like a senseless horse or mule*
that needs a bit and bridle to keep it under control."

[10]*Many sorrows come to the wicked,*
but unfailing love surrounds those who trust the LORD.
[11]*So rejoice in the LORD and be glad, all you who obey him!*
Shout for joy, all you whose hearts are pure!

■ Reflect on Psalm 32 and answer the following questions:

What two benefits are afforded those who live in complete honesty?
(see verse 2)

_____

What physical effects did David experience when he refused to confess his sin? (see verse 3)

_____

What is David's advice to all the godly, who apparently still sin? (see verse 6)

_____

David had been hiding from God, but then he confessed. Afterward, how does he describe God? (see verse 7)

_____

What two things does David say God does for him? (see verse 7)

_____

What promise of God does David rely on? (see verse 8)

_____

Whom does David say is surrounded by unfailing love? (see verse 10)

_____

Whom does David call to rejoice in the Lord, be glad, and shout for joy? (see verse 11)

_____

■ Answer the following questions to yourself:

Can you say that you live in "complete honesty"?

Are you in rebellion against God by refusing to confess your sins and be completely honest?

Do you feel more like you have to hide from God or that God is your hiding place?

Do you believe that God has forgiven all your confessed sin and put it out of sight?

Do you truly believe that God will lead you along the best pathway for your life?

Do you live as though you believe that God will advise you and watch over you?

Confession Is Good for the Soul

The Bible repeatedly affirms that confession is good for the soul. Below is a list of possible benefits from confession. Check any that you have experienced personally:

    ___ As you confess to others and they confess to you, you realize you are not alone in your sinfulness.

    ___ Confession releases you from the burden and misery of hiding your sin.

    ___ Confession helps you openly sort out your problems in the light of truth.

    ___ Confession affirms the reality of a situation and helps guard against deceiving yourself about your sin and its effects.

    ___ Confession enables you to receive comfort and help from others.

    ___ Confession leads to receiving forgiveness, which frees you from guilt.

    ___ Confession prompts you to take necessary action to deal with your sins.

■ Read James 5:16 (your memory verse for this week).

When we hide our sins from God and others, we invite sickness by our secrecy. This sickness of the soul can even take on physical forms at times. When God's people are willing to be open and honest about their sins, healing becomes possible. By breaking your silence and speaking the truth about yourself aloud to another person, you move out of the darkness and bring your secrets into the light. There is also the additional benefit that a confessed sin is a forgiven sin. When you have confessed everything on your conscience and are genuinely remorseful over your sin, you can experience the freedom that comes from knowing that God has forgiven you.

KEY THREE
SPEAK THE TRUTH

DAY 4

Verbalizing Your Confession

Today's focus is to encourage you to confess a hidden sin to God and to at least one other person. Many people say, "God knows my heart. I don't need to tell him out loud, much less tell anybody else." The Bible does say that God already knows your thoughts, but it also says that Christians should confess their sins to God and to each other. He doesn't tell you to confess for his benefit but for yours.

Sometimes people convince themselves that they've prayed and talked things over with God, and that's good enough. They figure, *As long as I know and God knows, why bother anybody else?* That ignores the simple, clear direction God has given us in James 5:16. Along with the healing that James speaks of, however, we also find that verbally expressing problems, faults, sins, disappointments, and weaknesses helps us sort out our thoughts and feelings. Confession allows you to hear your own story, told first person in your own terms. As you try to explain the thoughts and feelings that have been spinning in your mind, you may find that they are further clarified as you speak. At points you may find yourself saying, "I can't find the words," but as you continue to talk, the words gradually come, and with them a new understanding of your situation.

Yet while it is clear that God wants you to share openly within the Christian community, you should use wisdom in choosing a trustworthy confidant. Because we desire to be obedient and to cleanse our souls from the inside out, we confess our sins. But confession requires openness, which in turn requires vulnerability. In order to be vulnerable, however, a person needs to feel as though he can trust his confidant. Confession is an invitation to intimacy. Intimacy can only take place within trusting relationships. Therefore, you need to find someone who will keep what you share confidential and who will seek to restore you rather than merely condemn you. Use the following guidelines to help you identify individuals whom you may be able to trust with your confession.

Attributes of a Trustworthy Confidant

Humility

Does he have a proper view of himself in relation to God and others?

Does he exhibit pride, self-righteousness, or a judgmental spirit?

Is he more concerned about himself than about your needs and struggles?

Trustworthiness

Does she show that she values and respects your thoughts and concerns?

Have you ever seen her use privileged information against anyone else?

Have you ever seen her divulge privileged information about someone else?

Quiet godliness

Is he a Christian who seeks to please God in all that he does?

Does he inappropriately make a show of his faith?

Does he boast about what he knows and how he has helped others?

Stability

Is she an emotionally strong and secure person, able to give help to you freely without depending on you in return?

Does her life reflect that she understands how to live in a healthy and balanced way?

Does she have the time and energy to listen to your concerns?

Positiveness

Does he display a positive attitude toward life, demonstrating his ongoing faith in God's sovereignty and goodness?

Is he typically negative, fearful, or unhappy?

Are his conversations overshadowed by dark moods or pessimism?

Red Flags: Things to Avoid in a Confidant

Steer clear of someone who

may have a personal agenda that could be served by knowing what you have to share.

could serve *your* personal agenda, making it difficult for you to keep your motives for confession pure.

is extremely controlling and may become so regarding your problem.

is needy and emotionally unstable, exhibiting a pattern of latching on to others in order to meet his or her own needs.

may be sexually attractive to you or who may find you sexually attractive. This is especially true for those who are married. Do not confide in someone of the opposite sex other than your spouse.

■ Read James 1:5-8.

■ Ask God for wisdom as you consider whom you know that would make a trustworthy confidant. Write the name of anyone who comes to mind here:

_____

_____

_____

Guidelines for Confession

The following are some wise guidelines to remember as you confess your sins to another person:

Don't overburden your listeners. Have more than one person in whom you confide.

Be sensitive to their limits. Find out when they can meet and how much time they are able and willing to spend with you.

Don't hold expectations of them that are too high.

Think of them as friends, not therapists.

Don't throw out discretion.

Avoid giving explicit sexual details or unnecessary information, especially when it involves other people.

Don't stifle your true emotions.

Don't allow yourself to become completely dependent on them.

Ultimately you should learn to depend on God to get you through life.

KEY THREE
SPEAK THE TRUTH

DAY 5

Confession Builds Community

Why does God command us to confess our sins to each other? We have already noted that it is probably more for our benefit than for his, since God already knows our sins. Perhaps it is to develop a bond between believers, uniting them together in Christ. Speaking the truth to each other requires effort on our part—the effort of identifying beliefs, finding the words to describe them, and entrusting these words to another person. This process implies accountability, support, and unity. It ties other people into your life and you into the lives of other people. It causes the body of Christ to act as a single unit. A Zulu proverb says, "When a thorn pierces the foot, the whole body must bend over to pull it out." This saying graphically illustrates the body of Christ when it is working together properly.

■ Read Ephesians 4:15-16. Consider what role speaking the truth to each other plays in helping the body function well. Suppose the various parts of your physical body were to send false or incomplete information to the head or to the other parts of the body. What could happen if the eyes didn't report accurately what they saw, or if the ears didn't report truthfully what they heard?

_____

_____

_____

What kinds of conflicts and relational tragedies have you witnessed because people would not speak the truth to each other?

_____

_____

_____

Why do you think it is important to speak the truth to others and confess our sins to each other?

_____

_____

_____

■ Following is a list of reasons to speak the truth. As you read each reason, place a check beside it if you already mentioned it above:

    ___ God tells us to speak the truth to each other.

    ___ Sharing with each other sparks prayer.

    ___ Sharing with each other gives you the chance to receive encouragement from others.

    ___ Sharing with each other gives you the chance to draw from another person's wisdom and knowledge of Scripture.

    ___ Sharing with each other allows you to draw from the experiences of others.

    ___ Sharing with each other allows us to utilize the gifts God has given us to build up the body of Christ.

    ___ The reflections of others can give you fresh perspective.

___ Confessing wrongs against someone encourages people to give and receive forgiveness.

___ Confession reinforces our faith by reinforcing our belief in God's forgiveness through Jesus Christ.

___ Sharing with each other builds bridges and bonds between people and guards against loneliness and isolation.

Christ Calls Us to Confess Our Faith

As we mentioned earlier, obeying God's command to speak the truth also involves confessing our faith in Christ. When Jesus called people to follow him, he often told them to go home and tell their families of the wonderful things God did for them. He called them to confess him before others if he was going to confess them before his Father in heaven.

■ Look up the Bible references below. For each one, explain in your own words what the Bible says about the importance of confession, telling others of your faith in Christ, or telling others what God has done for you.

Romans 10:8-10:

_____

_____

Have you confessed with your mouth that Jesus is Lord?

_____

Will you now? _____ If so, confess it out loud.

1 John 1:9:

_____

_____

Have you confessed your sins to God? _____ If so, say, "I am forgiven."

Matthew 10:32-33 and Luke 12:8:

_____

_____

_____

_____

Have you acknowledged Jesus Christ as your Lord publicly here on earth? _____ If not, will you now? _____ To whom?

_____

Mark 5:18-20:

_____

_____

_____

Have you told your family and friends the wonderful things the Lord has done for you and how merciful God has been to you? _____ Will you now? _____ What will you tell them?

_____

_____

_____

_____

_____

Reviewing Key 3
What is the third key to spiritual renewal?

_____

As with last week, the biblical character who exemplifies this key for us is David. In your own words, describe David's negative experiences from refusing to confess his sins and then his positive experiences from confessing them:

_____

_____

_____

_____

_____

As you read Psalm 32, what did you learn about speaking the truth?

_____

_____

_____

Write out your memory verse from James 5:16 here:

_____

_____

_____

How have you confessed or spoken the truth in response to what you learned this week?

_____

_____

_____

_____

FOUR

Own it!

ACCEPT

RESPONSIBILITY

■

Memory Verse:
Galatians 6:5
*We are each
responsible for
our own conduct.*

KEY FOUR
ACCEPT RESPONSIBILITY

DAY *1*

Accepting Responsibility Paves the Way for Renewal

Before spiritual transformation can occur, you must be willing to accept responsibility for your life and allow it to be brought under God's rule. That means you must recognize who you really are, accept responsibility for what you have done, and then ask God to forgive and restore you. Once you do this, God will begin to work a miraculous process of renewal within you. As his child, you are a new creation, and God will continue to renew you along the way, using your past—no matter how bad or shameful—as the backdrop for a bright and glorious future.

In this lesson you will consider the example of **Peter.** As you examine his life as it is recorded in the Gospels, pay attention to the ways he uses each of the keys to spiritual renewal we have learned: seeking God and surrendering to him, seeing the truth, speaking the truth, and accepting responsibility. You will quickly find that Peter is a brash, impulsive, and emotional man. This proves to be his downfall; but when he sees the truth, confesses, and accepts responsibility for what he has done, Christ transforms his life. Christ even uses these very same qualities of Peter to further the gospel, turning his greatest weaknesses into his greatest strengths.

■ Read Luke 5:1-11.

How did Peter describe himself when he asked Jesus to go away? (see verse 8)

_____

Jesus didn't dispute Peter's self-assessment, but what prediction did he make about Peter? (see verse 10)

_____

■ Read Matthew 14:22-32. Look for indications of Peter's impulsiveness.

How did the disciples react when they saw Jesus walking on the water?

_____

After Jesus spoke to the disciples, who was willing to get out of the boat to meet him?

_____

What does this tell you about Peter's personality and behavior?

_____

_____

Peter tended to be a passionate and emotional man. While these characteristics often helped him to boldly follow Jesus, they could also act as weaknesses that Satan could exploit for his purposes. Jesus knew this about Peter, because Jesus could see him even more clearly than Peter could see himself. As you read the following passage, take note of the differences between Peter's expectations of himself and Jesus' expectations of Peter.

■ Read Luke 22:7-62.

KEY FOUR : *Accept Responsibility*

What did Jesus tell Peter that Satan wanted to do with him? (see verse 31)

_____

■ After Jesus said this to Peter, he told him, "But I have pleaded in prayer for you, Simon, that your faith should not fail. So when you have repented and turned to me again, strengthen and build up your brothers" (Luke 22:32). Did Jesus expect Peter to stand by him without faltering? _____ Circle the part of Jesus' statement that indicated he expected Peter to turn away from him.

What did Peter vow to Jesus? (see verse 33)

_____

_____

What did Jesus predict that Peter would do that very night?

_____

■ When the mob came to arrest Jesus, some disciples asked Jesus if they should fight against them with swords. One disciple even cut off the ear of the high priest's servant. Who do you think would do such a thing? Read John 18:10-11 to find out who it was.

While most of the other disciples scattered, Peter continued to fol-low Jesus—even into the courtyard of the high priest. Perhaps this was because he was still trying to carry out his promise not to leave Jesus even if everyone else did.

What are the verse references that record Peter's three denials of Jesus?

_____

How did Peter react when Jesus looked at him after his third denial?

_____

73

Given the fact that Jesus already knew what Peter would do, do you think he loved Peter any less after his failures? _____ Do you think Jesus was surprised by what happened? _____

This gives us a beautiful picture of how Christ views each of us. He saw Peter as he was, with his inherent strengths and weaknesses. Jesus knew that Peter's great passion and boldness could be redeemed and used to build up the church. But first, Peter had to see the truth about his own weaknesses so that he would depend on God's strength.

What have you seen about your own weaknesses that has caused you to depend on God's strength?

_____

_____

_____

_____

KEY FOUR
ACCEPT RESPONSIBILITY

DAY 2

Jesus' Response to Peter

As we continue our study of Luke 22:7-62, we see that Jesus didn't disown Peter because he denied him three times; but Jesus didn't ignore his failures either. Instead, he gave Peter a chance to accept responsibility for what he had done and be redeemed for service to God.

■ Read John 21:4-19. This passage describes an event that happened shortly after the resurrection of Jesus.

Jesus reenacted the miracle of filling the empty nets with fish. What promise would this call to mind for Peter? (If you're not sure, turn back to Luke 5:1-11.)

_____

_____

_____

Before Jesus could reaffirm Peter's calling as a disciple, he had to address and redeem Peter's denial that he even knew Jesus. What question did Jesus ask Peter three times in John 21:15-17?

_____

How many times had Peter denied Jesus? _____

By allowing Peter to reaffirm his love for him as many times as Peter had denied him, Jesus beautifully reinstated Peter to his position of leadership in the church.

After Jesus predicted what would happen at the end of Peter's life, what did he call Peter to do? (see verse 19)

_____

At this remark, what did Peter do? (see verses 20-21)

_____

Notice that Jesus didn't let Peter turn the attention from himself and ask about John. Jesus focused Peter's attention on his own responsibility. What was Peter's responsibility? (see verse 22)

_____

Peter's Transformation

Peter's entire personality didn't change after he had accepted responsibility for himself. But God did continue to change Peter, especially by means of the Holy Spirit, who came to fill the believ-

75

ers shortly after Jesus returned to his Father in heaven. Peter was then empowered to accomplish all that Jesus had called him to do.

■ Read Acts 2:1-41

How many of Jesus' followers were filled with the Holy Spirit that day?

_____

Who boldly stepped forward and preached the sermon that day? (see verse 14) _____

God is not a destroyer; he is a redeemer. He is not looking to eliminate the unique characteristics that make you the person you are; he wants to use them for his glory. In fact, when you accept responsibility for all that you *are*, you grasp another key to spiritual renewal.

Notice that God did not tell Peter never to mention that he had denied his Lord. No! Peter did not hide from what he had done; instead, he used it to show God's transforming power. Peter—the very one who had denied even knowing Jesus three times—became the great apostle and leader of the church. This gave hope of redemption to others. Anyone who was discouraged by his own failure to follow Jesus wholeheartedly could look at Peter's life and see that he too could still be used by God. Peter's life—his failures as well as his accomplishments—have become a valuable source of encouragement for countless others.

How does Jesus' treatment of Peter when he accepted responsibility for his failures encourage you to accept responsibility for your failures?

Owning Up to Your Past

God calls people to own up to their past, acknowledging their failures and sins. This doesn't mean he wants you to live in the past, but neither does it mean you should excuse wrongdoing just because it is in the past. Rather, God wants you to acknowledge the past—both the wrongs you have committed and the wrongs that have been committed against you—in such a way that you accept that it has been a part of your life. God is not looking to erase your unique history (though he does forgive our sins and remember them no more). Rather, he often chooses to use your experiences in a redeeming way.

■ In the paragraph above, underline what accepting responsibility for your past does *not* mean.

■ Now circle any phrases that describe what it *does* mean to accept responsibility for your past.

Who's to Blame?

Why is it that people so often are reluctant to accept responsibility for their lives? Perhaps it is because that would entail owning up to and dealing with sin and disobedience and the problems and consequences that have resulted. Human beings have inherited a sinful nature from our first parents—Adam and Eve. That sinful nature is always nudging us to point blame on others. People usually try to deflect the blame anywhere but toward their own heart.

■ Read Genesis 3:1-19.

Who chose to disobey God in this account?
    Just Adam   Just Eve   Both Adam and Eve

Who offered to accept responsibility for what he or she had done?
    Just Adam   Just Eve   Both Adam and Eve   Neither Adam nor Eve

Whom did Adam blame? _____

Whom did Eve blame? _____

Whom did God hold responsible?

_____

What were the results of their sin?

_____

_____

_____

_____

_____

As with Adam and Eve, God will not allow you to pass off blame to someone else regarding sins that you have committed. While others may influence you to sin, ultimately you are responsible for your choices and behavior. But there is good news: God has provided a way to deal with your sin once you have owned up to it. He has sent his Son to pay the price for your disobedience. While you may have to make restitution to others for wrongs you have committed, you can know that God has wiped your slate clean in his eyes.

■ Describe a time when you were confronted with your sin, but you tried to pass off the blame to others:

_____

_____

_____

_____

_____

What were some of the negative consequences of this refusal to accept responsibility?

_____

_____

_____

_____

_____

KEY FOUR
ACCEPT RESPONSIBILITY

DAY *3*

Weeds in the Garden

As we reflect on the effects of sin upon our lives and the responsibility we have to own up to it, we can envision our lives as a garden. God means for your garden to be fruitful, but whenever sin enters it—whether it is your sin or someone else's that has touched you—it will produce weeds. While you may or may not be at fault, you are responsible for your garden, and you must see to it that the weeds are removed. God can help you do this as you come to him. He will begin to reverse the curse of sin, pulling up the weeds that it has left behind in the garden of your life—both from you and from others.

One important thing to remember is that just because something is not your fault does not mean that it is not your responsibility. It is not enough to simply say, "That's not my fault." You cannot depend on others to come and remove all the sinful weeds they have planted in your life. At the same time, however, taking ownership of your garden does not mean that you take the blame for weeds you did not plant. You are responsible to remove them, but you are not to take the blame for them.

As you examine your garden, you may find that you do not have much weeding to do. This is often the case for those who walk closely with God, confess their sins regularly, and deal promptly with the sins others commit against them. But if you tend to blame others, avoid accepting responsibility for your own wrongdoing, and ignore the wrongs others commit against you, you may find your spiritual garden overrun with a tangle of old weeds.

■ Begin assessing the state of your garden by looking at one area of your life that tends to be a mess. Perhaps a particular relationship, or finances, or your performance at work. Identify the weeds that seem to be growing in that area of your life. Ask God to help you find these areas, so that they can begin to be changed. Ask yourself who is at fault for the problems you are now facing, and list them under the appropriate category below. You may find that you can quickly list the wrongs done to you by others, since many people rehearse this list quite often. But you also need to ask the more difficult question, What have I done or failed to do that has caused problems?

Wrongs Done to Me

1. _____

2. _____

3. _____

Wrongs I Have Committed

1. _____

2. _____

3. _____

As you have already learned, you need to accept responsibility for all these wrongs—these weeds in you garden—and begin to deal with them. You do this by confessing these wrongs to God and to others when appropriate, by acknowledging the real damage they have done, and by turning them over to God. You will learn more about turning them over to God in Key 5 (Grieve, Forgive, and Let Go). The following prayer can help you with this process.

> *Dear Father in heaven,*
> *I realize that you have given me life and that my life is my*
> *responsibility. Lord, I want to accept responsibility for my whole life.*
> *I know you want my life to be fruitful, but sin has infected my life—*
> *both by my hand and by the hands of others. Help me to accept*
> *responsibility to remove these weeds that have been sown in me.*

*Lord, I bring before you the unconfessed sins I have committed in the past. These are:*_____

_____ .

Lord, I confess that sometimes I have blamed others for my own disobedience to you. I now accept responsibility for these things. Please forgive me and fully restore the relationship between us, which has suffered because of my sin.

Lord, I bring before you the wrongs others have committed against me. You know that _____ *have sinned against me by* _____ .

Help me to release the anger or hurt I have been harboring against them, so that you can begin your work of restoring me and redeeming these wrongs. In Jesus' name I pray. Amen.

KEY FOUR
ACCEPT RESPONSIBILITY

DAY 4

Being Responsible for Your Conduct

■ Write out Galatians 6:4-5.

_____

_____

_____

God will hold you responsible for your conduct, and one day you will have to give account to him for your actions. Knowing this, it would be wise to consider your conduct now and take responsibility for what you do, so that you can correct things that are not right.

■ Review the following list of responsibilities that God has given to everyone. Assess how well you are managing each one, and circle the appropriate answer after each.

- Your body: taking care of your health; remaining sexually pure; and using your body as an instrument of righteousness.
  Great   OK   Need God's help   Really need God's help!

- Your emotions: being honest about your feelings; grieving your losses; managing your anger appropriately; rejoicing and weeping with others; allowing the joy of the Lord to be your strength when you face difficult trials; and trusting in God's Word rather than in your immediate feelings.
  Great   OK   Need God's help   Really need God's help!

- Your personality: understanding and accepting your unique personality while seeking God's help in changing you into Christ's image.
  Great   OK   Need God's help   Really need God's help!

- Your mind (intellect, natural abilities, and attitudes): holding the same humble attitude that Christ Jesus had; thinking on things that are true, noble, right, pure, lovely, admirable, excellent, or praiseworthy; allowing your mind to be controlled by the Spirit of God; allowing your mind to be renewed and guided by God's Word; loving God with all your mind; and using your intellect and natural abilities to advance God's kingdom.
  Great   OK   Need God's help   Really need God's help!

- Your spiritual life (including salvation, spiritual development, and gifts/talents): trusting in Jesus Christ as your Savior and Lord; pursuing holiness; participating in the body of Christ; remaining in Christ and bearing spiritual fruit; using your spiritual gifts to build up the body of Christ; and living by the Spirit and avoiding sinfulness.
  Great   OK   Need God's help   Really need God's help!

- Your attitude toward life: assessing what has happened to you and what you have done to others; dealing with these things honestly before God; recognizing that God seeks your good, not your harm, and that he can redeem everything—even those things that others have meant for evil; owning up to your actions and decisions; repenting of sin; refusing to blame others for your wrongs; facing your problems squarely; determining what part you have played in creating them; asking God to help you correct your mistakes and resolve your problems; and learning and growing through your problems.

Great   OK   Need God's help   Really need God's help!

■ Your moral conduct (including thought, word, and deed): accepting God's moral standards as revealed in the Bible as your personal standard for right and wrong; recognizing your sinfulness and inability to obey God's commands in your own strength; depending upon the Holy Spirit to help you turn from sin and live a holy life; seeking to please the Lord in everything; and confessing sin and receiving forgiveness through Christ Jesus.

Great   OK   Need God's help   Really need God's help!

■ Your relationships: seeking to live in peace with everyone; approaching those with whom you are not at peace and trying to settle the matter; confronting sin according to God's plan described in Matthew 18:15-17; refraining from slander, gossip, backbiting, and any other sin that undermines trust in relationships; and loving others as you love yourself.

Great   OK   Need God's help   Really need God's help!

■ Your roles: accepting God's guidelines and help for fulfilling the roles you have been given (husband, wife, parent, employer, employee, citizen, brother or sister in Christ, representative of Christ).

Great   OK   Need God's help   Really need God's help!

■ Your past: acknowledging what you were before you surrendered your life to Christ; owning up to the damage that you have done to others in the past; accepting the consequences of wrongdoing; and guarding against repeating your mistakes.

Great   OK   Need God's help   Really need God's help!

■ Your present state: knowing and accepting who you are in Christ (including seeing yourself as a new creation in Christ, knowing that your sins have been forgiven; and recognizing that you have been set apart for God); trusting God to provide for all your needs; praying to God for yourself and others; trusting in God's promises to you; and living as a child of the light.

Great   OK   Need God's help   Really need God's help!

■ Your possessions (including money, connections, material goods, and opportunities): regarding yourself as a manager of God's riches, not yours; handling your finances responsibly; using your resources to honor God and help others in need; valuing heavenly reward over earthly reward; remaining free from the love of money; regarding all your possessions as gifts from God; and refusing to use your resources in ways that harm others and displease God.

Great   OK   Need God's help   Really need God's help!

■ Your future: denying your selfish ambition and following Jesus for the rest of your life no matter what the cost; and being responsible with your gifts, talents, and time, so that you please God with all that he has given you.

Great   OK   Need God's help   Really need God's help!

■ Look back over this list and assess which areas need the most attention. Pray for God to help you become responsible in these areas. You may also want to discuss these things with a mature Christian to explore what the Bible has to say about each one. Always remember that God will give you the strength you need to be responsible in all that he has called you to do.

KEY FOUR
ACCEPT RESPONSIBILITY

DAY

Fulfilling Your Roles Responsibly

God has given his people specific guide-lines for how they are to treat each other and relate to each other.

Today you will consider what God's Word says about our responsibilities in specific roles and relationships.

■ For each of the relationships listed below, check any that apply to you. Then look up the Scripture passages cited to see what God says about each of these relationships. After each one, write out what you need to change in order to come into agreement with God's plan for that relationship. Pray that God will transform your life in that area.

Parent-Child _____

■ List the names of your parents or your children here:

_____

_____

You are called to be under the authority of your parents until you marry. When you marry, Christ says that you are to leave your mother and father and be united to your spouse (Matthew 19:5-6). But you are always called to honor your mother and father, even if you have married and are no longer under their authority.

■ Look up the following passages:
Deuteronomy 6:4-9
2 Corinthians 12:14
Ephesians 6:1-4

■ As parent or child, if you accept the responsibilities that God has laid out for you in his Word, sign your name here:

_____

■ Regarding your role as parent or child, list any specific commands you found in God's Word that you have not fulfilled as you should:

_____

_____

85

- Ask God to forgive you for your disobedience and neglect in this area. Ask him to help you fulfill these responsibilities from now on.

Employer-Employee _____

Some of these passages refer to slaves and masters. When these were written, slavery was an accepted part of life. These passages are not meant to condone slavery. We are not slaves to our work (although some people may feel like it), but we can still gain insights about work from these passages regarding the master-slave relationship.

Ephesians 6:5-9
Colossians 3:22-25
Philippians 2:14-16

- If you accept the responsibilities that God has laid out for you in his Word with regard to the employee-employer relationship, sign your name here:

  _____

- Regarding your role as employee or employer, list any specific commands you found in God's Word that you have not fulfilled as you should:

  _____

  _____

  _____

- Ask God to forgive you for your disobedience and neglect in this area. Ask him to help you fulfill these responsibilities from now on.

Husband-Wife _____

Some people will look at these verses and automatically focus on what their *spouse* is failing to do. Resist this urge! Instead, focus on the parts of the verses that apply to *you*. You are responsible to God for how *you* live as husband or wife.

Matthew 5:32; 19:19
1 Corinthians 7:3-5, 10-16, 39
Ephesians 5:21-33
Colossians 3:18-19

■ If you accept the responsibilities that God has laid out for you in his Word with regard to the husband-wife relationship, sign your name here:

_____

■ Regarding your role as husband or wife, list any specific commands you found in God's Word that you have not fulfilled as you should:

_____

_____

_____

■ Ask God to forgive you for your disobedience and neglect in this area. Ask him to help you fulfill these responsibilities from now on.

Christian-Christian _____

1 Corinthians 6:6-8
Galatians 6:10
1 Timothy 4:12; 6:2
1 Peter 4:8-10

■ If you accept the responsibilities that God has laid out for you in his Word with regard to your relationship with other Christians, sign your name here:

_____

■ Regarding your role as a fellow Christian, list any specific commands you found in God's Word that you have not fulfilled as you should:

_____

_____

_____

- Ask God to forgive you for your disobedience and neglect in this
  area. Ask him to help you fulfill these responsibilities from now on.

  Christian–Non-Christians (and strangers) _____

  Matthew 5:43-48; 22:39
  2 Corinthians 6:14-18
  Romans 12:17-21; 13:8-10

- If you accept the responsibilities that God has laid out for you in
  his Word with regard to your relationships with non-Christians,
  sign your name here:

  _____

- Regarding your role as a Christian witness, list any specific
  commands you found in God's Word that you have not fulfilled as
  you should.

  _____

  _____

  _____

- Ask God to forgive you for your disobedience and neglect in this
  area. Ask him to help you fulfill these responsibilities from now on.

  Christian-Government _____

  Romans 13:1-7
  1 Peter 2:17

- If you accept the responsibilities that God has laid out for you in
  his Word with regard to the government, sign your name here:

  _____

■ Regarding your role as a citizen, list any specific commands you found in God's Word that you have not fulfilled as you should.

_____

_____

_____

■ Ask God to forgive you for your disobedience and neglect in this area. Ask him to help you fulfill these responsibilities from now on.

Reviewing Key 4

What is the fourth key to spiritual renewal?

_____

The biblical character who exemplifies this key for us is Peter. In your own words, describe Peter's experiences regarding accepting responsibility for himself and his sins, and recount how his strengths and weaknesses were redeemed for God's glory.

_____

_____

_____

_____

How has this lesson helped you to accept responsibility for yourself and your actions?

_____

_____

_____

Write out your memory verse from Galatians 6:5 here:

_____

_____

Which type of relationship has been the most difficult for you regarding accepting the responsibilities God has placed on it?

_____

In what ways to do you plan to improve in this area?

_____

_____

_____

Release it!

G R I E V E ,

F O R G I V E ,

A N D

L E T   G O

■

Memory Verse:
Matthew 6:14
*If you forgive those
who sin against you,
your heavenly Father
will forgive you.
But if you refuse
to forgive others,
your Father will not
forgive your sins.*

KEY FIVE
GRIEVE, FORGIVE,
AND LET GO

DAY

God Calls Us to Forgive

The fifth key to spiritual renewal involves learning to grieve, forgive, and let go.

■ Look up the memory verse for this week (Matthew 6:14), and answer the following questions:

When you forgive others, what does God promise to do?

_____

_____

What warning does Jesus give those who refuse to forgive others?

_____

_____

On a scale of 1 to 10 ("1" being not important at all, "10" being of the utmost importance), how important would you say forgiveness is to you?

    1 2 3 4 5 6 7 8 9 10

Judging from this verse, how important would you say forgiveness is to God?

1　2　3　4　5　6　7　8　9　10

Lessons from Joseph

■ Read Genesis 37:2-36; 39:1–41:14. As you read, put yourself in the place of **Joseph,** and imagine how you would react to each of his experiences. As you empathize with Joseph, do the following: (1) Compile a list of all the people *who* wronged Joseph; (2) and list *how* Joseph was hurt by those who wronged him.

People who wronged Joseph:

_____

_____

_____

_____

How Joseph was hurt:

_____

_____

_____

_____

How long was Joseph a slave or prisoner because of the sins others committed against him? (see 37:2; 41:46)

_____

How long was Joseph in prison after the cup-bearer promised to tell Pharaoh of his plight? (see 40:23; 41:1)

_____

Did Joseph acknowledge that he had been treated unfairly? (see 40:14-15) _____

Was Joseph's life characterized by bitterness, hatred, vindictiveness, rage, depression, sickness, or doubt about God's sovereignty and goodness? _____

■ Reread Genesis 40:8; 41:15-16, 28, 32. According to these verses, how was Joseph's faith in God affected by the wrongs that others committed against him?

_____

_____

According to Genesis 41:38-40, Pharaoh could see the Spirit of God in Joseph because of his supernatural ability to interpret dreams. While the text does not tell us, it is probably also true that Joseph's lack of bitterness after such mistreatment contributed to the Pharaoh's recognition that the Spirit of God was in him.

Do you know people who have been mistreated and yet are free from bitterness, hatred, vindictiveness, rage, depression, sickness, or doubt? _____ If so, what connection do you see between their faith in God and their ability to forgive those who have sinned against them?

_____

_____

■ Read the rest of the story of Joseph and his brothers in Genesis 41:44–50:26. If Joseph had been carrying a grudge against his brothers, he could have paid them back at this point. What do Joseph's actions and attitude show regarding any bitterness he was harboring against his brothers?

_____

_____

In Genesis 50:16-17, Joseph's brothers finally admit that they have done many things wrong to him and have treated him badly. Judging from Joseph's words and actions, do you think Joseph waited for their admission of guilt before he forgave them? _____

Does this mean that Joseph excused or rationalized his brothers' actions instead of recognizing that they had done wrong? (see Genesis 50:20) _____

How do you think Joseph's attitude and actions (during his slavery, imprisonment, and rule over Egypt) might have been different if he had waited until his brothers admitted their guilt before he forgave them?

_____

_____

_____

Joseph's brothers sold him into slavery. In Genesis 50:18, they offer themselves as his slaves. How might Joseph have responded if he was looking to exact justice for himself?

_____

_____

_____

How do you think Joseph's story might have ended if he had refused to forgive those who sinned against him and had not trusted God's promises for his life?

_____

_____

_____

Do you believe the sins others commit against you can thwart God's promises to you? _____ How can the assurance of God's promises encourage you to forgive?

_____

_____

_____

KEY FIVE
GRIEVE, FORGIVE,
AND LET GO

DAY **2**

Clearing Your Ledger of Wrongs

■ People who harbor grudges and keep account of the wrongs others have done to them experience the negative effects of unforgiveness. Below is a checklist of common symptoms that can occur if you are harboring unforgiveness in your heart. Ask the Holy Spirit to help you discern if you are experiencing any of these symptoms of unforgiveness, and check any that apply.

___ Guilt (God has said he forgives us as we forgive others, so people who do not forgive recognize that they themselves are guilty before God)

___ Recurrent bouts of anger regarding some wrong done to you

___ Fantasies about how you will "pay them back" for what people have done to you

___ Growing bitterness

___ Feelings of resentment toward certain people whenever you experience any residual consequences of their wrongdoing toward you

___ Sarcasm and barbed words that seem to "slip out" with regard to particular people who have wronged you

___ Obsessive thoughts about how you were wronged, who wronged you, and the hurts you've incurred because of these wrongs

___ Desire for vengeance

___ Unexplained depression

Jesus taught his followers to pray, "Forgive us our sins, just as we have forgiven those who have sinned against us" (Matthew 6:12).

Jesus has called everyone to forgive, because at some time or another we will wrong others, and others will eventually wrong us. And when you are wronged, it is natural to feel that the person who wronged you *owes* you something. That feeling is natural, but God wants you to rise above this natural reaction and live by his Spirit. That means that you are to forgive. The Spirit of God will help you do this, just as he helped Joseph forgive his brothers.

Forgiveness can be thought of as a matter of spiritual accounting. When someone wrongs you, you take that into account. You might say that the person who wronged you is "on your list." That would be the internal list you keep in mind of the people you have not yet forgiven. Once someone is on your internal list, it is natural to think about how he has hurt you and what he may owe you because of his wrongdoing. As long as you keep account of his wrongs and think of him as owing you for what he has done wrong, you have not forgiven him.

When you forgive someone, you don't say that he never hurt you or that what he did was not wrong, nor do you pretend not to have any ill feelings because of what he has done to you. You forgive when you transfer his account over to God. You remove your personal claims against him from your own internal ledger and allow God to handle these matters, trusting in his wisdom to determine what must be done. This is where the concept of releasing it comes in. You don't negate the possible need for recompense; rather, you release the account to God.

■ The following exercise is intended to help you practice forgiveness. Just as you made two lists for Joseph, make two lists for yourself: (1) First list *who* has wronged you (those toward whom you still have ill feelings, even though you may have forgiven them and just be processing residual feelings); (2) then list *how* you were hurt by their wrongdoing.

Who hurt you:

_____

_____

KEY FIVE : *Grieve, Forgive, and Let Go*

_____

_____

How you were hurt:

_____

_____

_____

_____

Payment for Sins

Sins must be paid for; God's Word says so, and the human heart demands the same from others. Each time someone sins against us, we find ourselves asking, "How will this sin be paid for, and who will exact the payment?" Unlike us and our desire to see others pay for their wrongs, however, God has chosen to provide a way for our wrongs against him to be paid for by another—his own Son. When Jesus Christ died on the cross, our sins were nailed there with him. God acted with love, not vengeance, toward us, and he forgives us when we receive his generous offer. In response to his gracious forgiveness toward us, he calls us to forgive the sins that others have committed against us. It is natural to keep account of wrongs and hurts that others cause us, but then God calls us to turn these accounts over to him so that he can take care of the situation. That frees us to release these wrongs and move on.

It should be noted that biblical forgiveness is definitely *not* excusing or rationalizing the wrongs that others commit. The forgiveness that God calls us to extend to others is based on the forgiveness that God has extended to us. This forgiveness did not excuse sin; it is still accounted for. But the difference is that God is the one who has "settled the score," and he has done so in the perfect sacrifice of his Son.

■ Read Colossians 2:13-14. According to this verse, what did God do to cancel the debt that we owed him for our sins?

_____

■ Read Ephesians 1:7; 4:32.

How did God purchase our freedom from slavery to sin?

_____

_____

What does God call you to do in response to what he has done for you?

_____

_____

KEY FIVE
GRIEVE, FORGIVE, AND LET GO

DAY*3*

Reasons People Fail to Forgive

As we look at ourselves and the world around us, we will quickly see that forgiveness is not something that comes easily or automatically. We all have hurts that we continue to carry with us, since we refuse to release them to God. But if there is such pain with unforgiveness and great freedom when we turn our hurts over to God, why do we often refuse to forgive?

Some people fail to forgive because they refuse to honestly assess how they feel about being wronged. They minimize what others have done to them and fail to face up to the truth of their pain. But this failure to see the truth about themselves and others keeps them from forgiving these wrongs and releasing them to God. Examples can often be found in adults who were abused or neglected as children but who gloss over these wrongs, saying, "My parents did the best they could." Whether or not your parents did the best they could does not change whether or not they abused you. In this case, people may hesitate to admit the truth because it seems tantamount to saying that their parents did not love them.

When reviewing your past in order to forgive those who have wronged you, you should not seek to blame but, rather, to see the truth. If your parents were abusive, distant, or hypocritical, accept that truth. Then you can work toward transferring the *entire* account over to God. You cannot truly release something until you have faced the truth of it without distorting it in any way.

Is there someone you have tried to forgive but find that the person's account of wrongs keeps being reopened in your mind? _____
   If so, who is it?

It could be that the reason you seem unable to release this person's wrongs to God is because you have failed to face up to the truth about how you feel about his actions. You may have minimized his actions or tried to excuse them or pretend that he did not really wrong you.

■ If you are not sure whether this is the case, consider what might happen if you ever confronted, fully remembered, and faced the truth about the wrong the person did to you. Record your thoughts here:

_____

_____

_____

Some people refuse to forgive because they believe that to do so would be condoning the wrong that was done. They almost feel it is their duty *not* to forgive as a moral statement about the severity of the wrong that was done. These people may feel bound and burdened with the unforgiveness they carry with them through life, but they erroneously believe that they should not forgive those who wronged them.

God never minimizes or condones sin. If he did, he would not have sent his Son to die on the cross to pay for our sins, for he would not have needed to do so. Instead, God kept an account of all our wrongs, and then he nailed them to the cross of Christ. In ancient times, those who were crucified often had their charges—the reasons for their execution—nailed to the cross above them. When Jesus died on the cross, he paid the price for all the charges against us that were nailed to the cross with him. God allowed his Son to pay for our crimes. He allowed the blood of Jesus to pay for our debts to God.

■ Write out Colossians 3:13 here:

_____

_____

_____

According to this verse, why are you to forgive?

_____

_____

How did the Lord forgive you? Did he excuse your sin, or did he pay for your sins?

_____

Putting Forgiveness into Practice

■ Refer to the list you made of *who* sinned against you and *how* you were hurt by them. For each offense, use a separate piece of paper to write out the charges you hold against each person. Use the following format:

Forgiveness Transaction Form

To: The Lord
Re: A Wrong Done to Me

My complaint:

Write the name of the one who wronged you: _____

Write out what this person did that hurt you:

_____

_____

_____

Write out what this person cost you (respect, possessions, etc.):

_____

_____

Write out how you felt and still feel because of what this person did against you:

_____

_____

_____

Transfer of Accounts (When you are ready to release this hurt to God, pray the following prayer):

> *Dear Lord,*
> *You have commanded me to forgive others, just as you have forgiven me through the sacrifice of your Son, Jesus Christ. I choose to obey you, even though this is not easy for me. You listed all of my sins, then you nailed them to the cross so that Jesus' blood could pay for them. Help me to release this account over to you and not seek justice for my sake. Help me to trust that you are just and will carry out whatever punishment is necessary.*
>
> *Yet while I transfer this account to you, you know how I feel. You know the wounds that still remain as a result of this wrong. As I obey you by releasing this person from my debt, I pray that you will heal the hurts he has caused me. Help me to trust that you are willing and able to redeem me from the wrongs that have been done against me. If thoughts of vengeance recur, I pray that you will continually help me to release this person's account over to you. Amen.*

■ After you complete this process for each person on your list, draw a line through his or her name on your previous list. You may want to write over each one in red ink: "Account Transferred to God."

■ As you continue to feel the pain of these wrongs and recall the offense committed, reaffirm your decision in prayer, acknowledging what happened while choosing to transfer this person's account to God in obedience to his Word. Then praise God that your sins are forgiven as well.

KEY FIVE
**GRIEVE, FORGIVE,
AND LET GO**

DAY

Forgiveness Is an Ongoing Process
Forgiveness is not something you do only once in a while. You don't tuck this key away for those big occasions when someone does something terrible to you. This key should be used continually by everyone.

■ Read Matthew 18:21-22.

Jesus' call to forgive others is difficult enough when you are faced with hurtful, onetime offenses. It borders on the impossible, however, if you are living with a continuing pattern of unkindness, offense, or abuse. According to Jesus, however, Christians are commanded to practice forgiveness even toward those who repeat their offenses. Such an ongoing state of release requires an *attitude* of forgiveness, not simply an *act* of forgiveness. Forgiveness is release. As soon as a new account of wrong is opened up for someone in your heart, you need to begin the process of releasing it to the Lord. Just as you continually go to God to receive forgiveness for the sins you commit each day, you need to release others from the wrongs they commit against you every day.

■ Read the Lord's Prayer in Matthew 6:9-13. For the next week, pray this prayer each day. However, when you get to the sentence "Forgive us our sins just as we have forgiven those who have sinned against us," take time to list the sins you have committed that need God's forgiveness. Then list all the sins that have been committed against you that you are releasing to God. Make forgiveness of others as much a part of your daily prayers as asking God to forgive you.

Confrontation of Sin

Having noted that we must forgive those who continue in sin, however, we will now look at what God tells us about confronting such people. God does indeed call us to confront those who continue to sin and show them their need for a change of behavior.

■ Read Matthew 18:15-17.

What is the first step you should take when another believer sins against you?

_____

_____

What is the second step if he or she ignores your correction?

_____

_____

What is the third step if this person still refuses to listen?

_____

_____

What should the church do if someone refuses to heed its correction?

_____

_____

Forgiveness does not mean that you simply ignore sin and let people walk over you and others. God uses us to correct each other. These verses give clear guidelines for confronting sin and trying to correct it. Note that God does allow for the possibility that there may not be reconciliation. Even if you cannot be reconciled with the other person, however, you can still forgive the offending party from your heart.

■ Look at the names on your original list of those who have sinned against you. Which ones have you confronted about their wrongdoing?

_____

_____

If you didn't confront them, why not?

_____

_____

Releasing Your Desire for Vengeance
■ Write out Romans 12:17-19 here:

_____

_____

_____

_____

Who holds the authority to exact vengeance? _____

If you reserve the right to seek vengeance for yourself, whose place are you usurping? _____

How can this passage help you feel more comfortable turning your records of wrongdoing over to God?

_____

_____

Is there any sin that God's Word tells you that you are not to forgive? _____

When God's Word tells you to forgive, who benefits most by your act of forgiveness? (see Matthew 6:14-15; Mark 11:25; Luke 6:37)

_____

True forgiveness is an act of both faith and obedience. People do not forgive because they feel a lack of offense and anger toward those who have hurt them. People choose to forgive. And once they transfer their accounts to God, they begin the process of being released from their bitterness, pain, and anger over wrongdoing.

■ When you cannot forgive in your own strength, ask God to help you to forgive.

KEY FIVE
GRIEVE, FORGIVE, AND LET GO

DAY

Receiving Forgiveness and Making Amends

We have noted already that we are to forgive because God has forgiven us in Christ. In this lesson we want to delve a little deeper into the idea of being forgiven, both by God and by others we have wronged.

■ Read 1 John 1:9 again.

God has promised to forgive us of our sins when we confess them to him.

- Look up Micah 7:18-19. According to this verse, what does God do with the sins of his people?

  _____

  _____

- Read Hebrews 8:12.

  How often will God remember your sins after he has forgiven them?

  _____

As you memorize these scriptural promises and come to trust in them, you will begin to realize the forgiveness that God has already extended to you. Along with being forgiven by God, however, you can also find freedom in making amends or restitution for the wrongs you have done.

Just as you have a list of people who have wronged you, your conscience may have another list—one that tallies the wrongs you have done to others. This list may include things you have failed to do as well as things you have done.

- Read 1 Peter 3:15-16.

  How are Christians supposed to keep their consciences?

  _____

  What is one reason we should do this?

  _____

  _____

- Pray and ask the Holy Spirit to bring to your conscience any wrongs you have done to others that have not been resolved. These may be sins you have committed, promises you have broken, responsibilities you have shirked, or anything else that needs to be cleansed from your conscience. Then sit quietly for ten minutes. Make a list of anything that God brings to mind.

Things That Bother My Conscience

1._____

2._____

3._____

4._____

5._____

6._____

7._____

■ Look up the following refererences:

Luke 5:31-32
Acts 3:19
Acts 8:22
Acts 17:30
Acts 26:20
Romans 2:4
2 Corinthians 7:10

All of the verses above point out that true confession changes the heart, which in turn changes the behavior of the person. Today we tend to shy away from the idea of repentance. Perhaps it seems like an old-fashioned term. However, repentance is vital to experiencing true freedom from sin. While the blood of Jesus cleanses you from your guilt before God, the Holy Spirit convicts you of sin so that you can turn from it (repent). This turning from sin includes a desire to clean up the effects of your sin as much as you are able. As you admit where you have done wrong, God will lead you to try to make amends and restitution when possible.

■ Review your list of things that are on your conscience. Each item on that list will point to people who may have been hurt because of what you have done. Ask the Holy Spirit to bring these people to mind, and fill in the chart below.

Whom have you hurt by the wrongs you listed earlier?

1._____

2._____

3._____

4._____

5._____

6._____

7._____

An important consideration in making amends, however, is whether your efforts might injure the other person even more than before. You do not make amends simply to make yourself feel better, especially at the expense of others. You make amends because you are changing your course and because you are seeking to obey the teaching of Jesus. Make sure you are clear about what you are doing and why. Discuss it with a trusted friend or counselor who can pray with you and encourage you as to how you can make things right without creating further problems or pain for those you have hurt in the past. Below is a list of ways to make amends to someone you have wronged. Ask the Holy Spirit to show you if these or other ways will help you undo some of the damage you may have caused.

■ Make an apology. Say you are sorry for any trouble or pain you have caused.

■ Admit that you were wrong, or own up to your part in the problem.

■ Repay money you borrowed, or offer to pay for damages you caused.

■ Give back items that were borrowed and not returned.

■ Offer to repair anything you damaged that belonged to someone else.

■ Give back or pay for anything you have stolen.

■ Turn yourself over to law enforcement if you have broken the law.

■ Go with the person to a counselor or arbiter to help resolve a dispute.

■ Make a phone call or write a letter to communicate your remorse and repentance.

■ Publicly recant any gossip you spread, and make every attempt to undo the damage your gossip caused.

■ Pay back money owed that was cleared during a bankruptcy.

As you repent and make amends to the people on your list, cross off the debt of sin you were holding against yourself. As you try to right the wrongs you have done, you will grow in your enjoyment of forgiveness, and this will lead you farther along the road to spiritual renewal and transformation.

Reviewing Key 5
What is the fifth key to spiritual renewal?

_____

The biblical character who exemplifies this key for us is Joseph. In your own words, describe how Joseph demonstrated forgiveness:

_____

_____

_____

_____

Name one new idea about forgiveness that you learned from his example:

_____

_____

_____

Write out your memory verse from Matthew 6:14 here:

_____

_____

_____

Based on this verse and your work on this chapter, are you confident that you have forgiven all those for whom you kept account of
a wrong they had done to you? _____

If God were to forgive the same percentage of your sins that you
have forgiven others, what percentage of your sins would be forgiven? _____

What does this tell you about what you still need to do?

_____

_____

KEY

SIX

Redeem it!

TRANSFORM YOUR LIFE

■

Memory Verses:
2 Corinthians 1:3-4
All praise to the God and
Father of our Lord Jesus Christ.
He is the source of every mercy
and the God who comforts us.
He comforts us in all our troubles
so that we can comfort others.
When others are troubled,
we will be able to give them the
same comfort God has given us.

KEY SIX
TRANSFORM YOUR LIFE

DAY *1*

Lessons from Ruth

The sixth key to spiritual renewal is "Transform Your Life." The Bible character who exemplifies this key is **Ruth,** whose story is found in the book of the Bible that bears her name. The story takes place during the time when judges ruled over Israel, shortly before the time of the monarchy. When a famine struck Israel, an Israelite couple named Elimelech and Naomi moved to neighboring Moab. While there, Naomi's two sons married Moabite women, one of whom was Ruth. Eventually Naomi and her daughters-in-law were widowed, and Naomi made plans to return to Israel.

Ruth stood at a crossroads. Her husband was dead, and her mother-in-law was too old to bear another son to marry her, as was the custom. She had no children and no assurance that she ever would. Surely she was heartbroken with the loss of the man she loved, the man who was her only means of support in a society in which a woman's only protection and provision came from her father, husband, or close male relative.

Naomi urged her daughters-in-law to stay home in Moab in order to find other husbands among their own people. The one daughter-in-law did turn back, but Ruth would not hear of it. She determined to remain loyal to Naomi and to her God.

■ Write out Ruth 1:16 here:

_____

_____

_____

In the midst of her pain, Ruth chose to comfort Naomi and follow God. She did not know where that decision would lead, but she knew she was heading in the right direction. As a result, her life was transformed—redeemed! Ruth developed genuine faith in the God of Israel, and the law he had given his people provided for her redemption. In the law of Moses, the nearest male relative of a widow's deceased husband was responsible to marry her and raise up a family for his relative who had died. Ruth had such a person, who is sometimes called a family redeemer, and his named was Boaz. Over time, Boaz fell in love with Ruth and joyously fulfilled his role of redeemer. He married Ruth, and they had a son, Obed. Ruth was comforted by the fulfillment of God's promises. She laid the child in Naomi's lap and was able to comfort Naomi with the comfort she herself received from God.

■ Read the genealogy of Jesus Christ found in Matthew 1:1-17, and circle the names of all the women mentioned.

What great redemption story did Ruth become a part of because she was willing to redeem her tragic situation by comforting Naomi?

_____

_____

Because of her loyalty and faith in God, Ruth became one of the great heroines of the Scriptures. She allowed God to transform her life by turning pain into purpose and misery into a mission. She gave God her life, and he redeemed it.

Below are four ways we see the sixth key of spiritual renewal exemplified in Ruth's life:

■ Ruth chose to comfort someone else even in the midst of her own suffering.

■ Ruth determined to follow God no matter what that meant or where he led her.

■ Ruth laid claim to specific promises and provisions in God's Word.

■ Ruth watched God redeem her life by giving her an heir. This also allowed her to further comfort her mother-in-law, and her life became an inspiration to others regarding the power of God to redeem and transform a life.

As you progress spiritually, you can become an inspiration to others. When have you been in the midst of your own suffering and purposely intended to be a comfort to another?

_____

_____

_____

When did you determine to follow God, no matter what that meant or where he led you?

_____

_____

What difficult decisions have you had to make in order to follow God's will for your life?

_____

_____

_____

What specific promises and provisions in God's Word have you laid claim to that have transformed your life?

_____

_____

_____

Have you been able to comfort others with the comfort you received from God? _____ If so, how has your life become an example of God's power of transformation and redemption?

_____

_____

_____

Because of specific promises and provisions in God's Word, Ruth's life was redeemed, and she was greatly blessed. God can do the same with your life when you choose to trust and obey him. He will redeem you!

KEY SIX
TRANSFORM YOUR LIFE

DAY **2**

God Can Redeem Our Pain

Just as God provided a redeemer for Ruth and was able to use Ruth to comfort another in the midst of her pain, just as he was able to transform her life and make her an inspiration to others, God can do the same for you. But you must follow Ruth's example if you seek the kind of transformation and redemption she experienced. You must be willing to comfort others with the comfort you have received from God and appropriate his promises for your life.

One of the most reassuring promises in Scripture is found in Romans 8:28-29: "And we know that God causes everything to work together for the good of those who love God and are called according to his purpose for them. For God knew his people in advance, and he chose them to become like his Son, so that his Son would be the firstborn, with many brothers and sisters."

What does God cause to work together for the good of those who love him and are called according to his purpose for them?

_____

To whom does this promise apply?

_____

_____

Do you qualify? _____

Whom did God choose you to become like?

_____

If God chose his people to become like his Son and knows everything that will happen to them before it happens, and if he causes everything to work together for their good, is there any tragedy, any trial, any failure on your part, or anything else that God cannot redeem? _____

One of the great mysteries of life is God's ability to turn tragedy into good for those who love him and follow his will. He redeems the past—all of it—not just the nice parts! The gospel that saves your soul also promises to redeem and transform your life, making it an example to others. God causes *everything* in your life to accomplish his purpose, so that those who love him will become more and more like his Son.

Can this good news really be true? Can you accept it, believe it, and live as if it were happening? That is faith! And that is the kind of faith that will redeem your past, revolutionize your future, and transform your life and the lives of others.

■ Think of the worst thing that you have ever done or the worst thing that has happened in your life.

119

Do you believe that God can somehow cause that to work together with the rest of your life to produce something good? _____

If so, what change might this cause in your thoughts and behavior?

_____

_____

_____

_____

Claiming the promises of Romans 8:28-29 requires great faith—not in your own ability to transform your life, but in God's ability.

■ Look up the following verses:

Job 19:25
Psalm 19:14
Psalm 78:35
Isaiah 44:6
Isaiah 48:17
Isaiah 54:5

Who do these verses say is your redeemer?

_____

A New Perspective

When you realize that God is your Redeemer—that he desires to use all your experiences to make you more like Jesus Christ—you will gain a new attitude toward all of life, especially regarding your troubles and failures. This new perspective will give you hope and comfort as well. But, as we noted earlier, it takes faith in God's promises to gain this new attitude and hope.

■ Write out Hebrews 11:1 here:

_____

_____

_____

_____

■ If you truly trust God's promise to turn tragedy into good and make you more like his Son, take an inventory of all your difficult experiences and struggles. Ask God to fulfill his promise to you in these things. Also ask yourself who else has had similar experiences or struggles. God may possibly use you to comfort these people with the comfort you have received from him. For example, perhaps you have struggled with being overweight. God could use you to reach out to those who know the embarrassment and difficulties of being overweight. Write out your list of experiences and people below.

Pain or Struggle in Life	*People God May Comfort through Me*
1. _____	1. _____
2. _____	2. _____
3. _____	3. _____
4. _____	4. _____
5. _____	5. _____

The following prayer can help you bring your pain or struggles to God so that he can redeem them for good:

> *Dear Father in heaven,*
> *Please help me believe that you will redeem every aspect of my life and to live accordingly. Please help me to turn my past experiences and the comfort I receive from you into a source of comfort for others. Please bring people into my life who need that sort of comfort, and use me as you see fit. Thank you for causing everything to work together for good. Amen.*

KEY SIX
TRANSFORM YOUR LIFE

DAY *3*

Victory over Sin

God can redeem your past experiences, and Christ's resurrection from the dead demonstrates that he has the power to deliver you from your struggles and sins today, for he has already defeated the power of sin. When Jesus conquered sin and death, he defeated humanity's greatest source of shame and defeat. We still must wage the battle against our sin-inclined flesh, but we do so with the clear knowledge that he has already ensured ultimate victory.

■ Read Romans 6:5-14.

If we (Christians) have been united with Christ in his death, what can we be certain will also happen? (see 6:5)

_____

Why was our old sinful self crucified with Christ? (see 6:6)

_____

Why did Christ die? (see 6:10)

_____

For whose glory does he now live? _____

Romans 6:11 tells us that we should consider ourselves dead to sin and alive for the glory of God. How should this change the way we live? (see 6:12-13)

_____

_____

_____

■ Write out Romans 6:13 here:

_____

_____

_____

What is one example of a way that your body can be used as a tool for doing what is right instead of a tool for doing evil?

_____

_____

_____

While God has given you power over sin, he still allows you to choose whether you will yield yourself to him or to sin. You can still choose to serve your old master, sin, even though it no longer has any rightful claim on your life.

After Abraham Lincoln signed the Emancipation Proclamation, which legally set slaves free in this country, some slaves set out to find a new life of freedom. But many others did not appropriate the freedom that had been proclaimed on their behalf. They remained as slaves even though the law that held them in slavery had been overturned.

Think of the blood of Christ as your emancipation proclamation from slavery to sin. Are you like the former slaves who set out to live in newfound freedom, or are you more like the slaves who continued living as they had before?

_____

In what ways are you demonstrating either your freedom from or your enslavement to sin?

_____

_____

_____

■ If you still live much like you did before being united with Christ, seek God's help to break free from the power of sin. Study Romans

5–8, and pray with a mature Christian who can help you begin to live as dead to sin and alive to God in Christ Jesus.

KEY SIX
TRANSFORM YOUR LIFE

DAY 4

Living in the Hope of God's Redemption

Now that you are choosing to transform your life through God's power, you can learn to live in the light of God's intention to redeem you. Because you know that God is transforming the pain of your past into good things, you no longer need to look at your problems and ask *why*. Instead, you will ask *what*. *What can God do in the midst of this difficulty?* With this new attitude, each trial can be seen as a precious opportunity to see God work, for it is in your problems that you learn to appropriate the strength of God. You also learn to depend on God during these times, so your relationship with him will naturally deepen.

■ Read James 1:2-4.

What is the final outcome of those who learn to look at their trials in the way that James describes? (see 1:4)

_____

You may think that your story of redemption has to come to a "happy ending" before God can use you to comfort others. This is not so. God can use you in the midst of your problems and trials as a testimony to others that God is with you in the midst of troubled times and that he can be with them as well.

Without a doubt, stories of broken marriages restored, addictions overcome, or terminal illnesses cured are encouraging spiritual reports that can cause others to trust in God. But don't think that you are unable to help others until your "story" is complete. You can experience tremendous faith and spiritual renewal in the midst of your struggles, and others can be encouraged by your example along the way. In fact, for those who are still in pain, the testimony of your faith amidst your own pain is an even greater encouragement than the story of someone whose pain is a thing of the past.

What are some current struggles or troubles you are dealing with that God could use to show others his power and grace?

_____

_____

_____

_____

You may not have a happy ending to report just yet, but you can be confident that God will transform your difficulties and trials into something useful in the lives of others. The very process of spiritual renewal and transformation promises something far more than escape from your troubles. It promises change—inside your heart—in the midst of your troubles. And that change is the essence of true redemption.

When you begin to see every limitation in your life as a chance to invite God to do for you what you cannot do for yourself, you are taking hold of this key to spiritual renewal. If you long to find purpose in your pain and desire some good to arise from it, then ask God to redeem your circumstances and use you to help others. You cannot transform your life by yourself. This isn't a matter of pulling yourself up by your own spiritual bootstraps. God is the Redeemer, and he is willing and able to transform your life if you choose to allow him.

When you look to God to redeem your situation rather than get you out of it, he will usually move in and create opportunities for good that you would never have imagined possible. A good example of this would be the lead character in the *Shawshank Redemption*, where a man serving a life sentence for a murder he didn't commit "redeems" his time by using his skills to help others within the prison. Wherever you are, whatever your situation, you can transform your pain into an opportunity to help others. You start by looking at the people around you, identifying their needs, and doing whatever you can to help them.

What difficulty or struggle are you "stuck" in right now?

_____

_____

■ Take a moment and ask God, "How can I redeem this situation while I am still in the process of being delivered from it?" After a few minutes of silence, write down any thoughts God brings to your mind, and list any people you might be able to help:

_____

_____

_____

_____

All in God's Timing

The assurance that God can transform you even in the midst of your pain can give you consolation during difficult times. However, be sure that you don't skip over your own transformation or try to rush the process along in your eagerness to help others. God wants your life to be genuinely transformed—in his timing. When the time is right, God himself will bring people into your life whom you will be able to minister to with your life and your story.

Below are three things you should do while you are in the midst of your own trials:

■ *Take time to heal.* You will need time to process your pain, to grieve and express how you feel about it. You don't have to wait until the pain is gone for the process of redemption to begin. However, don't shortchange your own transformation in a rush to help someone else.

■ *Find others who share your struggles.* This might be your family, a
prayer group at your church, or a group designed to deal with
specific issues the members have in common. As you share what
you are going through, God can help you and perhaps help and
encourage others as well.

■ *Pray for God to help you and others through you.* Seek God's guidance
and wisdom, and be faithful to obey God's Word regarding your
particular situation. Also ask God to show you an outlet for helping
others.

KEY SIX
TRANSFORM YOUR LIFE

DAY

Sharing Your Story

As God redeems your past and you con-
sider ways to help others through your experiences, one habit you
can develop is verbally sharing what God has done for you—how
he has transformed your life. This includes telling others about your
salvation experience as well as telling them about the particular
struggles God has brought you through. This should not be born of
duty as much as it should be born of love—of God's love for you
and of your love for others. Revealing who you are and where
you've been epitomizes true love for others. However, it runs coun-
ter to our culture and to the principles of even many Christians.
Many people deliberately choose never to admit their struggles to
anyone else or to reveal how difficult it has been to overcome any
problems.

Are you willing to share God's love with others by sharing what God
has brought you through and delivered you from? _____

Who has benefitted from listening to your experiences of God's transforming power?

_____

_____

_____

What is something God has brought you through or delivered you from that you are unwilling to share with others who are struggling in similar ways?

_____

_____

Why are you unwilling to share this?

_____

_____

■ There are many reasons people hesitate to share what God has done in their lives. Which of the following reasons describe why you hesitate to share your testimony of how God has transformed and redeemed your life?

    ___ I don't know what to say or how to say it.
    ___ I don't think I am a good enough example of a Christian.
    ___ I'm too shy.
    ___ I don't want to push myself on anyone.
    ___ I'm afraid to reveal what God has brought me out of because I am ashamed of what I did and the kind of person I used to be.
    ___ Now that God has helped me, I don't really care about others who are still hurting.

You probably did not check the final option above. Most people who hesitate to share their redemption story usually do so because of shame or insecurity, forgetting that they are God's instrument to bring redemption and transformation to the lives of others.

It should be noted that there are some situations in which you may still be susceptible to falling back into old patterns of sin. When this is the case, be careful not to share with others in such a way that you may end up in a situation where, rather than lifting them up, they pull you down.

■ Look up Romans 10:13-14.

According to this verse, how has God chosen to spread his message of redemption?

_____

How are you helping to spread that message?

_____

_____

_____

How to Share Your Story

First Peter 3:14 says, "But even if you suffer for doing what is right, God will reward you for it. So don't be afraid and don't worry. Instead, you must worship Christ as Lord of your life. And if you are asked about your Christian hope, always be ready to explain it. But you must do this in a gentle and respectful way. . . ."

If you are hesitant to share your faith and experiences with others, know that this is common. At the same time, however, God says that fear and worry should not be allowed to keep you from sharing the reason for your hope in Christ, which is also the reason for the transformation you have experienced. Therefore, you need to be ready to share the reason for your hope. Preparation beforehand will help to dissipate some of your anxiety. Also remember that you have something positive and hopeful to share with them. As long as you share your personal experience of what God has done in your life, those who hear will be unable to dispute what you say. They may be able to dispute doctrine, but they cannot dispute a changed life, especially if the person sharing does so with gentleness and compassion.

■ When you tell the story of how you came to salvation and forgiveness for your sins, focus on three parts: what your life was like before you surrendered to Jesus, what brought you to Christ and how you came to believe, and the difference in your life since you have come to Christ. In the space below, write a brief description of each facet of your testimony.

What my life was like before I surrendered to Christ:

_____

_____

_____

_____

What brought me to Christ and how I came to believe in him:

_____

_____

_____

_____

How my life is different now that I have trusted in Christ and am following him:

_____

_____

_____

_____

■ You can also prepare to share how God has redeemed (or is redeeming) you from a particular struggle in your life. Again, briefly describe each of the things mentioned below:

What my life and beliefs were that led to the struggle:

_____

_____

_____

_____

What the struggle was and how it affected my life: (For this element, look for the kinds of experiences, feelings, and problems that may be a point of connection between you and your hearer.)

_____

_____

_____

_____

How God redeemed me (or is redeeming me) from the struggle and what he has taught (or is teaching) me through it:

_____

_____

_____

_____

God's desire is to transform your life in such a way that it will display his love and power to others. You have the privilege of seeing God turn your problems into a platform to reach others, your pain into purpose, and your misery into ministry. You play a vital role as you willingly pick up and use this sixth key to spiritual renewal.

Reviewing Key 6
What is the sixth key to spiritual renewal?

_____

The biblical character who exemplifies this key for us is Ruth. In your own words, describe the four ways Ruth exemplified transformation:

1. _____
2. _____
3. _____
4. _____

What kinds of pain have you experienced in which God has comforted you?

_____

_____

_____

What is one way God can use you to comfort others who are in this same situation?

_____

_____

_____

Write out your memory verses from 2 Corinthians 1:3-4 here:

_____

_____

_____

_____

What situation or trial can you seek to redeem by finding a way to do something good in the midst of it?

_____

_____

_____

What will you do?

_____

_____

_____

_____

Whom will you help by sharing your story of redemption and transformation?

_____

_____

KEY

SEVEN

Preserve it!

PRESERVE
SPIRITUAL
GAINS

■

Memory Verses:
Hebrews 10:35-36

Do not throw away
this confident trust
in the Lord,
no matter what happens.
Remember the great
reward it brings you!
Patient endurance is
what you need now,
so you will continue
to do God's will.
Then you will receive
all that he has promised.

KEY SEVEN
PRESERVE SPIRITUAL GAINS

DAY *1*

Lessons from the Apostle Paul

We would be remiss in our discussion of the keys to spiritual renewal if we failed to emphasize the absolute necessity of preserving spiritual gains—the seventh key. It would be a shame to come this far in your process of renewal only to watch yourself slip back into your old ways of living once again. In order to guard against this, you need to think of ways to firm up the new way of living you have found in Christ. And just as God has helped you grow spiritually, you can be assured that he will help to preserve the spiritual gains you have made and will continue to make. But you also need to make use of what God has already given you.

On his first missionary journey, the apostle **Paul** traveled through Asia Minor, spreading the good news of Jesus Christ. In city after city, Paul and Barnabas preached to those who had never heard of Jesus Christ. Spiritual renewal began, lives were transformed, and new groups of believers gathered together to worship God and grow in their newfound faith.

But Paul did not stop his work among these people after this first trip. He felt compelled to go on a second journey to revisit many of the churches he and Barnabas had established. The main purpose of this second journey was to preserve the spiritual gains they had made in the lives of the people there. On this journey, Paul strengthened the believers and taught them how to continue growing in their faith.

■ The following passage is taken from a letter Paul wrote to the Colossian believers. Read it as though Paul had written it to you personally. Take special note of the section that has been italicized.

> God in all his fullness was pleased to live in Christ, and by him God reconciled everything to himself. He made peace with everything in heaven and on earth by means of his blood on the cross. This includes you who were once so far away from God. You were his enemies, separated from him by your evil thoughts and actions, yet now he has brought you back as his friends. He has done this through his death on the cross in his own human body. As a result, he has brought you into the very presence of God, and you are holy and blameless as you stand before him without a single fault. *But you must continue to believe this truth and stand in it firmly. Don't drift away from the assurance you received when you heard the Good News.* (Colossians 1:19-23)

■ In the space below, write your personal response to Paul's letter. Be sure to acknowledge what Christ has already done for you, and affirm that you do "continue to believe this truth and stand in it firmly." Give specific examples of what you are doing or will do to make sure that you don't "drift away from the assurance you received when you heard the Good News."

Dear Paul,

_____

_____

_____

_____

_____

_____

_____

_____

_____

Sincerely,

_____

Paul knew that Christians do not live in a vacuum. All believers must take continual action to resist the pull of the world, their own sin-inclined flesh, and the forces of darkness, which are intent on leading astray the followers of Christ. The rest of this lesson will look at each of these three forces that works against our spiritual progress.

Spiritual Opposition from the World

When you endeavor to live a godly life and develop as God would have you, you will be going against the current of your culture and the world system that the Bible says is under the influence of Satan (the "god of this world").

■ Read John 15:18.

Does the world seem to love you or hate you?

_____

In what ways does it love you or hate you?

_____

_____

If you seem to fit right in with the world, what does that say about your spiritual distinctiveness, which is supposed to set you apart from the world?

_____

_____

139

■ Read James 1:27.

How does the world have the potential for corrupting you personally?

_____

_____

What kinds of things will you have to *do* to "refuse to let the world corrupt" you?

_____

_____

_____

■ Read 1 John 2:15-17.

What physical pleasures does the world entice you with?

_____

_____

What do you see that causes you to lust after it?

_____

_____

How does the world make you prideful in your possessions?

_____

_____

Which of these distractions holds the most sway over your life?

_____

_____

God calls you to love him with all your heart, soul, mind, and strength. Since the world is continually trying to draw you away from God, how often do you need to be concerned about spiritual preservation?

_____

Spiritual Opposition from Your Sin-Inclined Flesh

Even though you are a new creation in Christ Jesus, you still live in a physical body that is prone to sin if you do not walk by God's Spirit.

■ Read 1 Peter 2:11 and James 1:13-16.

Did you find that once you became a Christian your evil desires disappeared? _____

Most likely you still experience the evil desires, but with them you also have the consciousness of sin. In what ways have you experienced this inner conflict between your evil desires and God's Spirit, who lives within you?

_____

_____

_____

■ Read Romans 7:14-20.

These verses were penned by the apostle Paul. Notice that he wrote in the first person, admitting that this kind of inner conflict went on within him. If such a great saint experienced this kind of inner conflict, are you surprised that such an inner conflict goes on within you? _____

■ Later in the same letter, Paul wrote more about the sinful nature and the Spirit. Read Romans 8:5-11.

If you are a Christian, by whom are you controlled?

_____

■ Read Galatians 5:16-18.

When this passage addresses those who have "new life in the Holy Spirit," is it addressing Christians or non-Christians?

_____

How often are the sinful nature and the Spirit fighting each other?

_____

When are your choices free from the inner conflict between your sinful nature and the Holy Spirit?

_____

Given this insight into the conflict between your sinful nature and the Spirit, when can you disregard preserving the spiritual gains you have made?

_____

Spiritual Opposition from the Forces of Darkness

When you align yourself with God, you align yourself against God's archrival, Satan. As a Christian, you live in the midst of a great spiritual battle—one in which the enemy of your soul will continually oppose your spiritual progress.

■ Read Ephesians 6:11-12.

Against whom are Christians fighting?

_____

_____

_____

What does God call you to do to counteract this ongoing spiritual attack?

_____

_____

■ Read James 3:13-15.

How often do you think you need to attend to your spiritual walk if you are to live "a life of steady goodness"?

_____

Who motivates jealousy and selfish ambition?

_____

■ Read 1 John 4:1 and 2 John 1:7-8.

The two verses above show that people with whom you come into contact may be influenced by spiritual forces that oppose God. God says, "Watch out!" What do you need to do so that you are not deceived?

_____

_____

The Bible warns us that Satan is constantly seeking the destruction of believers. He is the great deceiver, continually working to lead Christians astray from God's truth. Satan's name means "the accuser," for he continually brings accusations against Christians for sins that God has already forgiven. He is also the tempter, continually trying to cause believers to relinquish the spiritual gains they have made. Lastly, Satan is always seeking to discredit or discourage all who align themselves with God.

Describe what you already do to combat the deception, accusations, and temptations that Satan repeatedly brings against you:

_____

_____

_____

■ Second Peter 1:4 says that God has given us his rich and wonderful promises so that through them we may share in God's divine nature and escape the decadence that is in the world. Below are three of

God's promises. Each one gives you bold assurance that will help you counteract the forces of the world, your sinful nature, and Satan. After each one, indicate which of the three forces it addresses.

Galatians 5:16 _____

John 16:33 _____

1 John 5:18 _____

KEY SEVEN
PRESERVE SPIRITUAL GAINS

DAY *2*

The Body of Christ

One means of preserving the spiritual gains you have made is to keep in close fellowship with other believers through the church, the body of Christ. Consider the clear instruction found in Hebrews 10:23-25:

> Without wavering, let us hold tightly to the hope we say we have, for God can be trusted to keep his promise. Think of ways to encourage one another to outbursts of love and good deeds. And let us not neglect our meeting together, as some people do, but encourage and warn each other, especially now that the day of his coming back again is drawing near.

This speaks of a close community of people who share a hope in the living God.

How well do you obey these verses and meet together to encourage other believers?

_____

List some ways you can actively encourage other Christians "to outbursts of love and good deeds."

_____

_____

_____

Do you regularly neglect to meet together with fellow believers?

_____

If so, when did you get out of the habit and why?

_____

_____

_____

If you are not part of a fellowship of believers who encourage and warn each other in the faith, you are missing out on a great blessing from God as well as disobeying his commands. The church is also important for helping you to preserve the spiritual gains you have made. What can you do to remedy your lack of fellowship with other believers?

_____

_____

_____

In 1 Corinthians 12, the apostle Paul used the metaphor of a body to describe the interaction of believers within the church. Jesus Christ is the head, each person is a part of the body, and the entire body is animated by one Spirit. Therefore, Paul appeals, we should recognize our need for each other and cooperate according to the will of God. This metaphor demonstrates that in order for any part to function, it must do so within the context of and in vital connection with Jesus Christ and other Christians.

■ Read 1 Corinthians 12:12-26.

If the body of Christ is a unit made up of many parts, is it possible to grow spiritually if you cut yourself off from vital connection with other believers? _____

According to verse 18, who put each part of the body where he wanted it to be? _____

What part do you play in the body of Christ?

_____

_____

■ Read 1 Corinthians 12:27-31.

God has given believers certain gifts in order to fulfill various roles within the church. Since no one has all of these gifts, the entire body is dependent on others who use their gifts to build up the entire body.

■ Reflect for a moment on the various tasks that need to be completed in your church. How do you see Paul's analogy of the body being worked out in your church?

_____

_____

_____

■ Read Ephesians 4:11-13.

According to verse 11, who are the gifts given to the church?

_____

_____

According to verse 12, what is their responsibility?

_____

_____

According to verse 13, what is the ultimate goal of these people and their gifts?

_____

_____

_____

How well do you share a unity of faith with your fellow believers?

_____

_____

How does knowledge of God's Son foster maturity in the Lord?

_____

_____

■ Read Ephesians 4:14-16.

Once we have gained maturity in the Lord through unity of faith and knowledge of God's Son, we should no longer be "forever changing our minds about what we believe." When you are challenged with ideas that contradict God's truth, how certain are you about your beliefs?

_____

_____

Accountability within the Body of Christ

The church is comprised of all those who have put their faith in Jesus Christ—all those who have been called out by God, set apart for his service, and gifted by his Holy Spirit.

God calls his church to be accountable to his Word but also accountable to each other. Matthew 18:15-17 gives specific guidance for confronting sin. Believers are told to go privately to the individual first, then to take two witnesses if necessary so that the truth of the matter can be confirmed. However, if the fellow believer still refuses to repent, the grievance is to be brought before the church. God has given the church authority to censure those who follow Christ but refuse to repent of sin.

It is within the context of interaction with other believers, especially those well versed in God's Word, that Christians learn to live holy lives and treat each other as God intended.

■ Read James 5:14-16.

While this passage is probably talking about physical health, the principle of accountability among believers is certainly applicable to spiritual health as well. How is this kind of interaction like or unlike your experience with other believers in your local church?

_____

_____

_____

God's Word shows us that each believer needs other believers in order to grow and preserve spiritual gains. While you may have reasons that explain why you shy away from actively participating in a local church, these do not excuse you from God's clear instruction. In addition to being part of corporate worship services, it is good to become accountable to a small group of fellow believers. This might be a group of men or women with whom you can share on a more personal basis. This might be a group formed around a common life experience, such as a group for parents, married couples, or people struggling with a particular area of sin. It may also be centered around a common goal or theme for the group, such as prayer, Bible study, or a specific topic for study and discussion. Whatever the connection, you need to be part of a group that is close enough to help each other examine their lives in comparison to God's Word and call each other to account.

If you are not actively part of a local church, are you willing to become an active member? _____

If you are not part of a small group, are you willing to join one?

_____

KEY SEVEN
PRESERVE SPIRITUAL GAINS

DAY*3*

Spiritual Disciplines

Preserving spiritual gains is a lot like taking care of your physical health. It is an ongoing process of doing the right things—a lifestyle of healthy living. To maintain physical health, you need a good diet, plenty of rest, clean air, and physical exercise. So it is with your spiritual health. You need to feed on God's Word, rest in the Lord (including rest by observing a Sabbath day each week), breathe deeply of God's Spirit (allowing him to rejuvenate and empower you), and exercise the gifts that God has given you.

The apostle Paul wrote the following words to a young pastor named Timothy, but they are also good instructions for all Christians: "Do not waste time arguing over godless ideas and old wives' tales. Spend your time and energy in training yourself for spiritual fitness. Physical exercise has some value, but spiritual exercise is much more important, for it promises a reward in both this life and the next" (1 Timothy 4:7-8).

■ List what you do to maintain both physical fitness and spiritual fitness:

Physical Fitness:

_____

_____

_____

_____

Spiritual Fitness:

_____

_____

_____

_____

If you do many things to contribute toward your physical fitness, what kinds of benefits do you see in your physical health?

_____

_____

If you do few things that contribute toward your physical fitness, what effect does this have on your vitality, health, and general sense of physical well-being?

_____

_____

If you do many things to contribute toward your spiritual fitness, what kinds of benefits do you see in your spiritual health and fitness?

_____

_____

If you do few things that contribute toward your spiritual fitness, what effect does this have on your vitality, health, and general sense of spiritual well-being?

_____

_____

You probably have enough evidence from your own life to convince you that the ongoing health and vitality of your physical body is related to how well you take care of it and maintain it with exercise, diet, and rest. The same is true of your spiritual health, as you learned from 1 Timothy 4:7-8. Today you will look at numerous ways you can supplement and enhance your spiritual health.

Before we begin explaining these ways to improve your spiritual health, however, we should note that we are not talking about earning your salvation or gaining favor with God by works. Remember, you enter God's kingdom by being born again, as Jesus described in John 3:3. Anyone who is born has life; however, the quality of that life is determined by how well a person cares for his or her physical health. Likewise, your salvation is complete on the basis of what Jesus Christ did on the cross and your faith in his completed work. However, the quality of that spiritual life will be determined by how well you care for your spiritual health. We call practices designed to build up your spiritual health *spiritual disciplines.*

Following are ten spiritual disciplines highlighted in *Seven Keys to Spiritual Renewal* and the *Spiritual Renewal Bible.* Just as you have not done every physical exercise, you may be unfamiliar with some of these spiritual disciplines. Don't get discouraged if you have not tried these before. Instead, consider the potential each one has to enhance your spiritual walk. Look up the reference for each one, and then answer the questions following.

■ *Silence*
Psalm 46:10

When have you removed yourself from the din of the world and listened for God's voice?

_____

_____

What did you learn from the exercise?

_____

_____

_____

■ *Fasting*
Matthew 6:16-17

If you have ever fasted for spiritual purposes, what did you learn from the experience?

_____

_____

Before you fast, you should read about its purpose and the various ways to fast, especially since this discipline generates physical effects as well. You should also consult your physician before you begin.

■ *Service*
1 Corinthians 16:15-16

How do you actively serve God, your fellow Christians, or your community?

_____

_____

_____

If you could make a real difference in the world by serving others, what kind of difference would you like to make? Whom would you like to help?

_____

_____

_____

What could you do today to serve others?

_____

_____

■ *Repentance and Confession*
1 John 1:9-10

Do you have a regular time of personal reflection that includes self-examination, repentance, and confession of sins? _____

Do you confess your sins to others as God commands? _____

■ *Stewardship*
2 Corinthians 8:6-15

Stewardship means being careful to manage wisely and obediently the resources (time, money, etc.) God has given you. Part of this wise and obedient management involves giving offerings to the Lord's work and to those in need. How are you fulfilling God's commands regarding your resources?

_____

_____

_____

Look up the following verses and reflect on their meaning for you:

Malachi 3:10-12
Matthew 5:42
Matthew 6:3
Luke 6:38
Luke 12:33-34
2 Corinthians 9:6-8

After reflecting on these verses, write down any changes that need to be made in your attitude or habits toward giving:

_____

_____

_____

■ *Prayer*
Ephesians 6:18

How often do you pray?

_____

What do you pray for?

_____

_____

_____

How do your times of prayer help you to grow spiritually?

_____

_____

_____

How might you improve your prayer life? Check any of the following that could be of help:

___ Learn more about prayer to motivate you and instruct you.
___ Set aside a regular period of time to pray.
___ Write out your prayers so that you do not become distracted.
___ Find a partner with whom to pray on a regular basis and make a commitment to do so.
___ Other:

- *Worship*
  Psalm 100:2; John 4:23-24

How do you worship God?

_____

_____

_____

Have you ever experienced joyful and powerful times of worship where you could sense God's presence as you worshiped him?

_____

Check any of the following that may be of help in improving your worship:

    ___ Learn more about worship.
    ___ Participate in leading worship (if you are gifted to do so).
    ___ Listen to various kinds of music and spiritual songs that can help you to worship.
    ___ Participate in forms of worship that are different from your usual style.
    ___ Other:

■ *Spiritual Friendship*
John 15:13; 3 John 1:2

How do your friends help you grow in your faith?

_____

_____

How do you help your friends grow in their faith?

_____

_____

_____

■ *Solitude*
Mark 6:31-32

Jesus took his disciples aside to a quiet place so that they could be refreshed. When do you take time to get away from the hectic pace of your daily routine to spend time in solitude with Jesus?

_____

_____

How does this change your spiritual perspective?

_____

_____

_____

■ *Bible Study and Meditation*
Joshua 1:8; 2 Timothy 2:15

How does the amount of time you devote to Bible study compare to the amount of time you spend watching television or participating in your favorite hobby?

_____

_____

If you need to improve your study of the Scriptures, how will you do this?

_____

_____

_____

Some Christians cringe at the thought of practicing meditation, because it has come to be associated with Eastern religions and New Age practices. But God does not call us to empty our minds as many of these religions do. God calls us to meditate on his Word. Meditation is directed thought—in this case, thought about what God has told us in his Word.

■ Look up the following verses and note what God wants us to meditate upon:

Joshua 1:8

_____

Psalm 48:9

_____

Psalm 77:11-12

_____

Psalm 119:27

_____

Psalm 119:148

_____

Psalm 143:5

_____

Philippians 4:8

_____

Now that you have reviewed several disciplines of the faith, consider how you can implement them in your own spiritual walk. But just as you would not start doing every physical exercise possible at the start of a new exercise regimen, don't set your sights too high in your aim to incorporate these spiritual disciplines into your life. Choose one that you would like to add to your daily routine. Once you have incorporated that one, look to add the others as the Holy Spirit leads you. Any of these spiritual disciplines that you practice can assist you as you seek to preserve your spiritual gains.

KEY SEVEN
PRESERVE SPIRITUAL GAINS

DAY

Spiritual Gifts

We have seen how spiritual disciplines can help you grow in your spiritual walk. They can help you change, make you more able to reach out to others, and continue the process of redemption, both in your life and in the lives of those God places in your path. Perhaps the most effective way to help others, however, is to employ the spiritual gifts God has given you.

We have already touched on the topic of spiritual gifts when we learned about the importance of participating in a local church. This lesson will delve more deeply into the topic of spiritual gifts, however, and you will consider what gifts God has given you to share with others.

God's Word reveals that all Christians are members of Christ's body, a metaphor Paul uses to describe the church. God has uniquely gifted each person to fulfill a particular function in the body of Christ. Just as each part of the physical body was designed by God for a specific purpose, you have been designed to perform a particular function in the body of Christ. God has created you and gifted you to minister to others according to his design.

You can explore the subject of spiritual gifts in Romans 12:3-8 and 1 Corinthians 12–14. These chapters list the following gifts:

Discernment of Spirits	Apostleship/Ministry
Serving	Evangelism
Helping	Prophecy
Mercy	Teaching
Hospitality	Pastoring
Healing	Leadership
Exhortation	Administration
Giving	Miracles
Wisdom	Tongues
Knowledge	Interpretation of Tongues
Faith	

■ Circle any of these gifts that you think God may have given you to serve others within the church.

■ For each one you circled, give an example of when you exercised this gift and saw someone within the church benefit.

_____

_____

_____

_____

_____

Earnestly Desire the Most Helpful Gifts

The topic of spiritual gifts has been the source of controversy in some church denominations, causing some Christians to avoid the subject altogether. Regardless of your particular denominational persuasion, however, as a Christian, you dare not disregard Paul's statement at the end of his discourse on spiritual gifts. He writes, "And in any event, you should desire the most helpful gifts" (1 Corinthians 12:31). Paul was settling controversy that had arisen in his day regarding the use and misuse of spiritual gifts. Nonetheless, at the end of his discourse, he urges Christians to desire spiritual gifts that will be the most helpful to the body of Christ.

■ From the list given above, choose any spiritual gifts that you feel are both desireable to you and especially necessary in your church. List them below, giving your reasons for selecting each and the ways in which they would help the church:

1. _____

_____

_____

2. _____

_____

_____

3. _____

_____

■ In the space below, compose a prayer asking God to provide your church with people who possess these gifts if it is his will. Ask him to show you if he has chosen and equipped you to serve your church through any of these gifts:

Dear Father in heaven,

_____

_____

_____

_____

_____

_____. *Amen.*

Manage Your Spiritual Gifts Well
■ Read 1 Peter 4:10-11.

It is important to use your gifts and manage them well for several reasons. First, by knowing your gifts, you know yourself better. This self-awareness will enable you to make wise choices about how to use your time, talent, and resources most effectively for the kingdom of God. Recognizing your gifts and then putting them to work for God's kingdom provides genuine fulfillment and accomplishes the things God has called you to do.

You can determine some of your spiritual gifts by reflecting on how God has designed you and the talents he has given you. Some questions you might ask yourself are: What do you like to do best? or What are you most successful at doing? One of the joys of exploring your spiritual gifts is discovering that your gifts are usually what you enjoy doing most. Jesus' parable of the man who left bags of gold for his servants to invest while he was gone (found in Matthew 25:14-30) suggests that God has given each of us various talents and called us to invest them to the best of our ability. So even if you are not sure a particular talent is a "spiritual gift," you are well within the boundaries of God's will to use all your talents to help others in the body of Christ and to take the gospel to unbelievers.

■ List the talents you possess:

_____

_____

_____

How might these talents be used to build up the body of Christ or to advance the kingdom of God?

_____

_____

_____

What could you do today to begin using your talents for God?

_____

_____

_____

If you have not explored developing your spiritual gifts, it would be both wise and rewarding for you to sit down with some Christian friends and discuss the topic of spiritual gifts. Study God's Word regarding this issue, and pray for God to show you how to discover and use your spiritual gifts to build up the church. By using these gifts, you will help to solidify and preserve spiritual gains made by you and by others.

PRESERVE SPIRITUAL GAINS

DAY *5*

Persevering in God's Word

So far we have looked at three aspects of the Christian life that will help you in spiritual preservation: (1) participating in the body of Christ, (2) practicing spiritual disciplines, and (3) discovering and using your spiritual gifts. The fourth and final aspect of spiritual preservation we will look at is perseverance—simply continuing to practice your faith and enduring in it, no matter what.

One of the keys to perseverance is staying true to God's Word. The apostle Paul knew that he could not just teach the truth once and assume everyone would stay on track. He knew that his teachings had to be reinforced over and over again. That is why he made his second missionary journey—to strengthen and encourage the churches he and Barnabas had established.

Regarding spiritual matters, many people have a tendency to drift like a boat in a current. That is why the Bible tells all believers to persevere in God's Word. Hebrews 2:1 says: "So we must listen very carefully to the truth we have heard, or we may drift away from it." Another time Paul warned Timothy, a young pastor, "Keep a close watch on yourself and on your teaching. Stay true to what is right, and God will save you and those who hear you" (1 Timothy 4:16).

This image of a boat floating with a current is helpful for recognizing how you can combat this tendency in your spiritual walk as well. Just as a sailboat must continually be steered toward the destination and redirected when it veers off course, so, too, you need to continually check the direction of your life to make sure it is headed where God wants it to go. There are many things that can cause you to veer off course—difficulties, conflicts, temptations—so you need a spiritual compass to keep you on track. That compass is the Bible. Any time you begin to direct your life in reaction to the events and beliefs swirling around you, you will drift off course. But the Bible will give you absolute truth that you can use to guide your life to the destination that God intended for you.

Describe an occasion when you took your eyes off God's truth and drifted off course in life:

_____

_____

_____

How did God's Word help you get back on course? Or, how *could* his Word have helped you?

_____

_____

_____

_____

Persevering in Times of Suffering

Christians should expect that they will encounter trials and times of suffering. God calls them to persevere during these times, despite the difficulties surrounding them. The Christians addressed in the New Testament book of Hebrews endured terrible suffering. They were publicly humiliated, ridiculed, beaten, and thrown into jail, and their property was confiscated. But they were commended and encouraged to persevere. The writer to the Hebrews told them:

> You accepted it with joy. You knew you had better things waiting for you in eternity. Do not throw away this confident trust in the Lord, no matter what happens. Remember the great reward it brings you! Patient endurance is what you need now, so you will continue to do God's will. Then you will receive all that he has promised. (Hebrews 10:34-36)

While you may never know the kind of persecution these Christians suffered, there will be times you will have to be patient and endure until God's promises are fulfilled. Understanding this will help you continue growing spiritually no matter what.

What did the writer to the Hebrews say these Christians needed in order to continue to do God's will in the midst of suffering?

_____

When have you needed patient endurance to continue doing the will of God in adverse circumstances?

_____

_____

_____

Waiting for the Harvest

Another image we can use to help us persevere in our faith is that of harvest. The Bible often speaks of waiting until "due season" to receive a harvest of blessing for obeying God. Today, however, people are used to instant gratification, and this can cause us to give up in our spiritual walk if we allow it. Spiritual growth comes in seasons, but we must always be faithful in season and out of season to ensure a bountiful harvest. You must keep on doing the right things, even though you don't see the harvest immediately.

Faith and patience in the context of Christian community are vital to preserving your spiritual gains. This idea is expressed in the letter to the Hebrews:

> Our great desire is that you will keep right on loving others as long as life lasts, in order to make certain that what you hope for will come true. Then you will not become spiritually dull and indifferent. Instead, you will follow the example of those who are going to inherit God's promises because of their faith and patience. (Hebrews 6:11-12)

God's Word says to "keep right on loving others" with the promise that "you will not become spiritually dull and indifferent." What else can you "keep right on doing" that will prevent you from becoming spiritually dull and indifferent?

_____

_____

_____

Who can help keep you accountable in carrying out these things?

_____

Reviewing Key 7
What is the seventh key to spiritual renewal?

_____

The biblical character who exemplifies this key for us is the apostle Paul on his second missionary journey. In your own words, describe how Paul's efforts on his second missionary journey exemplified how we must preserve spiritual gains:

_____

_____

_____

Write out your memory verses from Hebrews 10:35-36 here:

_____

_____

_____

What are the four aspects of the Christian life that will help you preserve spiritual gains (see Day 5)?

1._____

2._____

3._____

4._____

REVIEW

OF THE

Seven Keys

The goal of this workbook is to bring about spiritual renewal and transformation in your life. This doesn't take place simply by knowing about these keys, but rather, by using them. Therefore, what you have learned must be put into practice before it will make a difference in your life. This final week the lessons will help you to look back, review each key, and decide how you will continue to use these keys in everyday life.

The Seven Keys to Spiritual Renewal

- Key 1: Seek God and Surrender to Him

- Key 2: See the Truth

- Key 3: Speak the Truth

- Key 4: Accept Responsibility

- Key 5: Grieve, Forgive, and Let Go

- Key 6: Transform Your Life

- Key 7: Preserve Spiritual Gains

Because we have laid out these keys in sequential order, you might automatically assume that they are steps that must always be followed in progression to get to some plateau of spiritual development. Using this mental picture, one would think that in order to use Key 5 ("Grieve, Forgive, and Let Go") in a given situation, you would first have to go through Keys 1 through 4. This is not necessarily so. While the principles build on each other, each of the keys should become so familiar to you that you can begin to recognize when you need to forgive and go directly to Key 5 to deal with a situation where unforgiveness is an issue for you. While going through a checklist of all seven keys can be a spiritually healthy review, it is not always necessary.

Since we want you to become proficient at using all seven of these keys as needed in your life, try thinking of the seven keys as being on a circular key ring in your pocket. You have all seven available to you to help you when you encounter a difficult situation. Each time you face a difficulty, you can use any of the keys you have at your disposal. Some situations may present a combination of issues that seems to lock you out of the kind of spiritual vitality you seek. In those situations you may need to try all seven keys until you find the right combination that opens the doorway to a breakthrough in your particular situation.

During this last week, we hope to assist you not only in reviewing each key but in assessing when you might need it, where you are spiritually regarding the key, and how this key can help change your life.

Your spiritual growth is never complete. This workbook may come to an end, but its conclusion may leave you with a list of spiritual issues you want to explore, questions you need answered, and areas of your life that you need to align with God's will. The pages following will help you assess all of this in relation to each of the seven keys and determine what you need to do to continue on your quest for spiritual renewal and transformation.

KEY ONE

Key Phrase: Seek God and Surrender to Him

Biblical Example: Zacchaeus. He went seeking Jesus and ended up surrendering his entire life to him that day.

Memory Verse: Pray like this: Our Father in heaven, may your name be honored. May your Kingdom come soon. May your will be done here on earth, just as it is in heaven. (Matthew 6:9-10)

Personal Application and Review: The person who is fully using this key should be able to make the following statements:

■ I am seeking God's kingdom first in my life and seeking his righteousness.

■ I recognize God as my king; therefore, I willingly bring my life under his righteous rule.

■ Like Jesus, I can honestly pray, "Father, I want your will, not mine."

■ When I cannot control a situation, I surrender; I let go and let God handle it.

■ I continually submit myself to God's way of doing things instead of insisting on my own way.

■ Instead of trying to change everyone else, I surrender to God and ask him to change me.

■ I will continually look to see what areas of my life need to be surrendered to God daily.

■ I will humble myself before God and submit my life to his command.

■ I will surrender my independence and join with others in God's kingdom.

In the space below, write out all of the statements listed above that you can truly agree with at this time:

_____

_____

_____

_____

_____

_____

_____

_____

_____

_____

In what ways are you seeking God?

_____

_____

_____

_____

Spiritual renewal begins with a personal relationship with Jesus
Christ. Describe your relationship with Jesus Christ and how it has
changed as a result of this workbook:

_____

_____

_____

_____

_____

Surrendering to God means giving up control, which can be fright-
ening. What still makes you afraid to surrender some areas of your
life to God?

_____

_____

_____

What areas of your life do you still control (or try to control)?

_____

_____

_____

God calls you to surrender every area of your life to him. Reflect on each of the following and describe specific ways God is calling you to surrender this area of your life to his control:

Your reputation and public image:

_____

_____

_____

_____

Your moral conduct:

_____

_____

_____

_____

Your thoughts and fantasies:

_____

_____

_____

Your personal life and actions that others never see:

_____

_____

_____

_____

Your career:

_____

_____

_____

_____

Your commitments to other people:

_____

_____

_____

_____

Your relationships (family, church, community, work, friendships):

_____

_____

_____

_____

Your emotions (fear, worry, anger, sorrow, etc.):

_____

_____

_____

_____

Your finances and material possessions:

_____

_____

_____

_____

Your future:

_____

_____

_____

_____

Your pride:

_____

_____

_____

_____

Another aspect of this first key is daily surrender to God, in which you "let go and let God" take care of things that are beyond your control and allow God's will to guide you. In what particular situations do you need to let go and allow God's will to direct you?

_____

_____

_____

_____

Jesus modeled surrender for us by doing only what pleased his Father in heaven. What are some areas of your life that do not line up with God's will?

_____

_____

_____

Compose a prayer asking God to help you follow Jesus' example in these areas:

Dear Father in heaven,

_____

_____

_____

_____. *Amen.*

All people are slaves to one of two possible masters: sin or righteousness. In what ways do your actions reflect your new master, righteousness?

_____

_____

_____

In what ways do you still act like you are a slave to sin?

_____

_____

_____

Surrender also means being content amidst your circumstances. What are some concrete ways you can exhibit contentment in Christ?

_____

_____

_____

KEY TWO

Key Phrase: See the Truth

Biblical Example: David. The prophet Nathan challenged him to face his sinful actions and deal with them.

Memory Verse: Search me, O God, and know my heart; test me and know my thoughts. Point out anything in me that offends you, and lead me along the path of everlasting life. (Psalm 139:23-24)

Personal Application and Review: The person who is fully using this key should be able to make the following statements:

- I am willing to see the truth as God sees it.

- I am willing to see my own problems in the light of truth.

- I recognize that my criticisms of others are often clues to my own failures.

- I am willing to hear honest feedback about my life that can help me identify my blind spots and correct my errors.

- I will view my actions in light of God's grace and mercy toward me.

- I will see myself for who I really am, but I will also remember who I am in Christ and what God has done for me.

- I will honestly recognize my weaknesses.

In the space below, write out all of the statements listed above that you can truly agree with at this time:

_____

_____

_____

_____

_____

_____

_____

If you are a Christian, you are to walk in the light because God has delivered you from the kingdom of darkness. Describe how you used to walk in darkness and what it means for you to walk in the light.

_____

_____

_____

_____

_____

David was willing to call out, "Search me, O God." How do you feel about asking God to search your heart right now? What hidden sins need God's light to shine on them so that they can be dealt with?

_____

_____

_____

_____

When you are spiritually farsighted, you see others' faults, but you are blind to your own. In what areas of life are you often spiritually farsighted?

_____

_____

_____

_____

Do you struggle with any addictive or compulsive habits? _____
If so, how might this be your way of avoiding the pain of seeing the truth in your life?

_____

_____

_____

How does seeing the truth about God's remedy for sin encourage you to see the truth about yourself?

_____

_____

_____

_____

In addition to ignoring his own sin, David closed his eyes to obvious problems within his family, which resulted in terrible complications. What are some problems in your life that seem so overwhelming that you simply cannot bear to look at them squarely and deal with them?

_____

_____

_____

_____

_____

Regarding your own sins and the problems that need to be dealt with in your family, who is someone you can talk to in order to get a clearer perspective on these situations and what must be done about them?

_____

When will you talk with this person about these things?

_____

KEY THREE

Key Phrase: Speak the Truth

Biblical Example: David. He confessed his sin with Bathsheba in Psalm 51 and asked for God's forgiveness.

Memory Verse: Confess your sins to each other and pray for each other so that you may be healed. (James 5:16)

Personal Application and Review: The person who is fully using this key should be able to make the following statements:

- I submit myself to God's standards of right and wrong.

- I acknowledge that I am sinning any time my thoughts or conduct do not line up with God's standard.

- I confess my sins out loud to God.

- I confess my sins to another person.

- I will speak the truth about what others have done to me and how their sins have hurt me.

- I will no longer try to keep secrets from God or from those to whom I make myself accountable.

- I confess Jesus Christ as my Lord, and he will confess me before his Father in heaven.

- I confess my praise and worship of God openly.

In the space below, write the statements listed above that you can truly agree with at this time:

_____

_____

_____

_____

_____

_____

How do you regularly practice confession in your life?

_____

_____

_____

_____

When you experience an inner conviction of some sin in your life, what is your response?

_____

_____

_____

_____

How does this compare with what the Bible says you should do?

_____

_____

_____

How do you need to change your response in order to agree with what God calls you to do?

_____

_____

_____

God wants you to confess your love for him and praise him. In the space following, confess your love for God in writing. Be sure to praise God for who he is and all that he has done for you.

_____

_____

_____

_____

_____

_____

Describe ways in which you have rationalized, exaggerated, told half-truths, or lied in the past in order to avoid speaking the whole truth about yourself.

_____

_____

_____

_____

_____

How has your failure to speak the truth hurt other people?

_____

_____

_____

_____

How has it hurt you?

_____

_____

_____

_____

What can you do to help yourself speak the truth?

_____

_____

_____

_____

What causes you to hesitate when you need to confess something or speak the truth?

_____

_____

_____

_____

What negative or harmful side effects have you experienced as a result of not confessing a sin?

_____

_____

_____

_____

The Bible shows us that confession is good for the soul. What benefits can you look forward to when you learn to speak the truth?

_____

_____

_____

_____

What sin do you still need to confess? Begin by writing a prayer of confession to God:

Dear Father in heaven,

_____

_____

_____

_____

_____. *Amen.*

Who is another person to whom you can confess this sin?

_____

When will you talk with this person and confess your sin?

_____

Biblical confession that brings healing takes place within a Christian community. How can you participate in such a community so that you will have the proper context for ongoing confession?

_____

_____

_____

KEY FOUR

Key Phrase: Accept Responsibility

Biblical Example: Peter. He denied Jesus, but he was restored to ministry after he was given an opportunity to accept responsibility for his actions.

Memory Verse: We are each responsible for our own conduct. (Galatians 6:5)

Personal Application and Review: The person who is fully using this key should be able to make the following statements:

- I accept responsibility for my God-given roles.

- By the grace of God, I will carry my own load.

- I accept responsibility to take care of my mind and body.

- I accept responsibility for my emotions, honestly recognizing my feelings and dealing with them appropriately.

REVIEW : *The Seven Keys*

- I accept responsibility for my commitments and promises.

- I accept responsibility for my actions and attitudes, along with their consequences.

- I will not blame others for my sins and actions in life.

- I will not blame myself for the actions of others.

- I will not overburden myself with the responsibilities of others.

  In the space below, write the statements listed above that you can truly agree with at this time:

  _____

  _____

  _____

  _____

  _____

  _____

  _____

  Peter denied Jesus three times, but when he accepted responsibility for his failure, Jesus restored him to ministry. When have you accepted responsibility for your sins or failures and witnessed God's restoration as a result?

  _____

  _____

  _____

  _____

  _____

185

What is something you still need to accept responsibility for? How can you demonstrate your acceptance of responsibility in this area?

_____

_____

_____

_____

_____

Whom have you blamed instead of accepting responsibility for your life?

_____

_____

In what areas of your life do you require the most help with carrying out your responsibilities?

_____

_____

_____

_____

_____

Name one way in which this workbook has helped you accept responsibility for something. What were the results of your acceptance?

_____

_____

_____

_____

_____

_____

KEY FIVE

Key Phrase: Grieve, Forgive, and Let Go

Biblical Example: Joseph. He forgave his brothers for selling him as a slave.

Memory Verse: If you forgive those who sin against you, your heavenly Father will forgive you. But if you refuse to forgive others, your Father will not forgive your sins. (Matthew 6:14-15)

Personal Application and Review: The person who is fully using this key should be able to make the following statements:

- I recognize that if I refuse to forgive others, I am cutting myself off from God's forgiveness for my sins.

- I will acknowledge the wrongs done against me without excusing or justifying them.

- I will take account of the wrongs done against me, but I will quickly turn those accounts over to God.

- I accept Christ's forgiveness for my sins, which were nailed to the cross.

- I will extend the forgiveness of Christ to those who have sinned against me.

- I will not hold grudges against those who have hurt me, nor will I seek vengeance against them.

- Whenever I feel vindictive, I will turn the case over to God and allow him to deal with the situation.

- I will do my best to make amends or restitution for my wrongdoing, except when doing so would hurt others even more.

■ By the grace of God, I will forgive repeatedly.

■ I will forgive others just as God in Christ forgave me—not because they deserve it.

In the space below, write the statements listed above that you can truly agree with at this time:

_____

_____

_____

_____

_____

_____

_____

_____

For whom do you keep a strict account of wrongs that they have committed against you?

_____

_____

_____

_____

The Bible tells us that genuine love keeps no record of wrongs. Regarding the people listed above, whose accounts are you willing to turn over to God?

_____

_____

_____

God has given clear guidelines for confronting those who have wronged us. Of those people you listed in your answer above, whom have you confronted lovingly and in a biblical manner?

_____

_____

_____

How and when will you confront those whom you have not yet confronted?

_____

_____

_____

_____

Upon whom do you seek vengeance for wrongs they committed against you?

_____

_____

_____

The Bible tells us that vengeance belongs to God alone. How will you deal with your desire for vengeance?

_____

_____

_____

_____

What wrongs have you committed that you want to release from your conscience by making amends?

_____

_____

_____

_____

What do you need to do to make amends and release them?

_____

_____

_____

_____

As we have learned, God calls us to grieve, forgive, and let go of wrongs committed—both by others toward us and by us toward others. What are the benefits of being forgiving and forgiven like this?

_____

_____

_____

_____

KEY SIX

Key Phrase: Transform Your Life

Biblical Example: Ruth. She received a new life and great blessings by trusting God with her tragedies.

Memory Verse: All praise to the God and Father of our Lord Jesus Christ. He is the source of every mercy and the God who comforts us. He comforts us in all our troubles so that we can comfort others. When others are troubled, we will be able to give them the same comfort God has given us. (2 Corinthians 1:3-4)

Personal Application and Review: The person who is fully using this key should be able to make the following statements:

- I will trust that God is causing everything to work together for good, since I love him and am being conformed to the image of his Son, Jesus Christ.

- I choose not to wallow in self-pity but to look for ways God can redeem any situation.

- When things go wrong, I will stop asking God, "Why?" and start asking, "What do you want me to do in this situation?"

- When experiences in life humble me, I will strive to have a servant's heart.

- When I experience pain or problems, I will look for ways that this can help me identify with others' pain.

- When I am hurting and God is comforting me, I will comfort others in the way he comforted me.

- I will share my story with others to lead them to Jesus and to help them.

- I will look for ways that God can turn my pain into purpose and my misery into ministry.

In the space below, write the statements listed above that you can truly agree with at this time:

_____

_____

_____

_____

_____

_____

How has God already redeemed aspects of your life that you might have thought impossible to redeem?

_____

_____

_____

_____

What is one problem you are encountering right now in which you cannot see any good resulting from it?

_____

_____

_____

_____

_____

What will help you believe that God can and will work some ultimate good from this situation?

_____

_____

_____

_____

_____

What pain have you experienced in life that God could use to help you identify with someone else?

_____

_____

_____

_____

_____

Whom can you identify with as a result of your pain?

_____

_____

_____

_____

_____

What difficult situation do you find yourself in where you cannot change the circumstances but you can change your attitude and actions within the circumstances?

_____

_____

_____

_____

_____

What do you think God might be calling you to do to redeem your situation and show others God's love?

_____

_____

_____

_____

KEY SEVEN

Key Phrase: Preserve Spiritual Gains

Biblical Example: The apostle Paul. He embarked on his second missionary journey for the purpose of strengthening and encouraging the churches he helped establish.

193

Memory Verse: Do not throw away this confident trust in the Lord, no matter what happens. Remember the great reward it brings you! Patient endurance is what you need now, so you will continue to do God's will. Then you will receive all that he has promised. (Hebrews 10:35-36)

Personal Application and Review: The person who is fully using this key should be able to make the following statements:

- I recognize that I must continually strive to preserve my spiritual gains so that I do not drift away from the truth.

- I recognize that I must continually strive to preserve my spiritual gains because I experience continual resistance from the world, my own sin-inclined flesh, and the forces of darkness.

- I commit myself to actively participate in Christian fellowship.

- I will be accountable to other believers who share my faith in Jesus Christ and live according to God's truths revealed in the Bible.

- I see the value of practicing spiritual disciplines to deepen my relationship with God, though I realize that these things do not earn salvation or favor with God.

- I will seek to discover and use my spiritual gifts in order to build up the body of Christ and gain fulfillment.

- I know that there will be trials and troubles in this life, during which I must persevere in my faith.

- I know that it is by patient endurance that I will inherit God's promises.

- I will continually read God's Word and adjust my life to stay true to it.

In the space below, write the statements listed above that you can truly agree with at this time:

_____

_____

_____

_____

_____

_____

_____

_____

We can make conscious efforts toward preserving the spiritual gains we have made. One thing we can do is actively participate in a local church. Describe your involvement in the local church and how it helps you stay true to God's Word:

_____

_____

_____

_____

Developing close relationships with other believers can continue our efforts toward preserving our spiritual gains. How are you developing these sorts of relationships, and how has it helped your Christian walk?

_____

_____

_____

_____

To whom do you hold yourself accountable in an effort to ensure spiritual progress?

_____

_____

_____

Which spiritual disciplines have you practiced, and how have they helped you in your Christian walk?

_____

_____

_____

_____

_____

Which spiritual disciplines do you plan to practice in the future, and what do you hope to gain by them?

_____

_____

_____

_____

The practice of spiritual disciplines can be done for many reasons. Ultimately, however, God wants you to practice the spiritual disciplines out of love for him and a desire to grow closer to him. He does not want you to practice them for show, or because someone is pressuring you, or even because you are hoping to gain favor with God.

What are your reasons (good or bad) for practicing the spiritual disciplines?

_____

_____

_____

_____

_____

What do you believe are your spiritual gifts?

_____

_____

_____

_____

How do you use these to build up the body of Christ?

_____

_____

_____

_____

What can you do to further explore your spiritual gifts and use them within your local church?

_____

_____

_____

All believers must persevere in God's Word, making certain that their actions and beliefs line up with God's desires. How do you do this on an ongoing basis?

_____

_____

_____

For your entire earthly life you will be susceptible to the pull of the world, your sin-inclined flesh, and Satan. What is your plan to continually resist the pull of the world so that you can preserve your spiritual gains?

_____

_____

_____

_____

What is your plan to continually resist the pull of your sinful flesh?

_____

_____

_____

_____

What is your plan to continually resist the pull of the forces of darkness?

_____

_____

_____

_____

_____

Spiritual preservation takes ongoing commitment to continue on in your faith. Describe how you intend to live out this commitment with patient endurance.

_____

_____

_____

_____

Concluding Remarks

Our prayer has been that you would use this workbook to make a real difference in your life. We would appreciate hearing what God is doing in your life as a result of what you have learned and begun to do through this workbook. You can contact us at:

New Life Clinics
570 Glenneyre Ave, Suite 107
Laguna Beach, CA 92651

Our prayers go with you as you continue to use the Seven Keys to Spiritual Renewal.

DEVOTIONAL READINGS FROM THE

Spiritual Renewal Bible

∎

The following devotionals are taken from the *Spiritual Renewal Bible*. While they have been selected to corre- spond generally with your lesson each day, there may be some that correspond more closely than others. If you enjoy these devo- tionals, we suggest that you go on to read the rest of them that are found in the *Spiritual Renewal Bible*.

- **Key One: Seek God and Surrender to Him**

  Day 1: The Starting Point (Psalm 111:1-10)

  Where do we start in search of spiritual renewal? We must start with the realization that spiritual renewal comes from God. It is not so much that we seek the experience of spiritual renewal as we seek the one who renews our spirits.

  When people came to Jesus to have their needs met, very often he redirected their thinking. He taught them to lift their eyes from their own daily necessities and seek God first. He told them, "He will give you all you need from day to day if you live for him and make the Kingdom of God your primary concern" (Matthew 6:33). We cannot seek the Kingdom of God without bowing to the King himself. In the same way, the psalmist encourages his listeners to look to God first, who will then meet their needs: "Who can forget the wonders he performs? How gracious and merciful is our LORD! He gives food to those who trust him; he always remembers his covenant" (Psalm 111:4-5).

  So it is with our spiritual hunger. Spiritual renewal does not come from seeking spiritual renewal. That will simply result in a temporary emotional high that lacks the true substance that God can provide. Instead, we must seek God and surrender to his rule in our lives.

- **Key One: Seek God and Surrender to Him**

  Day 2: Surrendering in Times of Suffering (Job 19:8-27)

  When we experience pain and loss because of something beyond our control, we may feel as if God is our enemy. But the anger and confusion that result don't have to separate us from God. We may never grasp why God allows such torment, but we can surrender to him, trusting that a time is coming when we will understand his will for us.

During his suffering, Job also experienced feelings of bitterness toward God, remarking, "God has blocked my way and plunged my path into darkness. He has stripped me of my honor. . . . He has destroyed my hope. . . . He counts me as an enemy. . . . My close friends abhor me. Those I loved have turned against me. I have been reduced to skin and bones and have escaped death by the skin of my teeth" (Job 19:8-20).

Despite Job's confusion and pain, however, he was able to conclude his near despair with a statement of faith in God. He said, "But as for me, I know that my Redeemer lives, and that he will stand upon the earth at last. And after my body has decayed, yet in my body I will see God!" (Job 19:25-26). Like Job, we must remember that God is on our side even when we don't understand our suffering, and we can surrender to him in trust.

- **Key One: Seek God and Surrender to Him**
  Day 3: Our Prime Example of Humility (Philippians 2:5-9)

Our prime example for surrender to God is Jesus Christ. Christ's humility can be easily seen as he continually sought his heavenly Father in prayer and relinquished his will to him.

The apostle Paul wrote, "Your attitude should be the same that Christ Jesus had. Though he was God, he did not demand and cling to his rights as God. He made himself nothing; he took the humble position of a slave and appeared in human form. And in human form he obediently humbled himself even further by dying a criminal's death on a cross. Because of this, God raised him up to the heights of heaven and gave him a name that is above every other name" (Philippians 2:5-9). In a similar vein, the author of Hebrews wrote, "[Jesus] was willing to die a shameful death on the cross because of the joy he knew would be his afterward. Now he is seated in the place of highest honor beside God's throne in heaven" (Hebrews 12:2).

Note the progression: Jesus humbled himself; yet it was because of this that God raised him up to the heights of heaven. Humility was a key element in Jesus' life as he accomplished God's will for fallen humanity. If we are surrender to God and his will for us, we need to be humble as well. Jesus did not pray solely for his own will. He humbly prayed for his Father's will to be done. We, too, ought to pray, "Father, I want your will, not mine." This is the mark of true humility and the beginning of spiritual renewal.

■ **Key One: Seek God and Surrender to Him**
Day 4: The Promise of Positive Change (Titus 2:11-14)

When we seek God and surrender to him, we receive renewed hope for positive change in our lives. Of course, we may have doubts about our ability to change, and these are reasonable doubts because we may have failed in the past to make the changes we needed to make. But, through surrender, we can be assured that real change is possible because God himself promises to help us change.

Paul recognized that God can and will help us change, so he wrote to Titus, "For the grace of God has been revealed, bringing salvation to all people. And we are instructed to turn from godless living and sinful pleasures. . . . [Jesus Christ] gave his life to free us from every kind of sin, to cleanse us, and to make us his very own people, totally committed to doing what is right" (Titus 2:11-14).

God has promised to save us and make us his people! Meanwhile, he is in the process of rescuing us from our bondage to sin. Let us cooperate with God's plans for our salvation by surrendering to him and turning from sinful pleasures.

■ **Key One: Seek God and Surrender to Him**
Day 5: Rest for the Weary Soul (Matthew 11:27-30)

There are plenty of roads that promise to lead us to spiritual renewal and transformation, but not all of them lead in the right direction. Some of us have grown weary going down one such road and then another . . . and then another. We exhaust ourselves seeking spiritual refreshment. Many of us have worked hard at building a good life, but instead of joy in the journey, we feel weighted down by life. We need rest for our souls.

Proverbs tells us, "There is a path before each person that seems right, but it ends in death" (Proverbs 14:12). The fact that a way seems right doesn't mean it is leading toward true spiritual renewal; it could be leading to a dead end. Those of us who have taken many paths but still find ourselves weary need to come to Jesus. He said, "Come to me, all of you who are weary and carry heavy burdens, and I will give you rest. Take my yoke upon you. Let me teach you, because I am humble and gentle, and you will find rest for your souls. For my yoke fits perfectly, and the burden I give you is light" (Matthew 11:28-30).

Any spiritual path that does not lead us to Jesus Christ will not lead to true spiritual renewal—no matter how right it seems. In fact, Jesus Christ himself is our way (John 14:6). The burden he calls us to bear on our journey is light, and the yoke of his expectations fits us perfectly. When we do this, Jesus promises rest for our souls. Then we can experience true spiritual renewal.

■ **Key Two: See the Truth**
Day 1: Humility and Wisdom (Mark 14:3-9)

The disciples' negative response to this woman's actions and Jesus' rebuke of them show us that we need God's help to see the truth in every situation. This requires our humble willingness to receive God's wisdom, and our openness to the Holy Spirit, who promises to guide us into all truth.

Solomon wrote, "Getting wisdom is the most important thing you can do! And whatever else you do, get good judgment" (Proverbs 4:7). The apostle Paul prayed constantly for fellow believers, "asking God, the glorious Father of our Lord Jesus Christ, to give you spiritual wisdom and understanding, so that you might grow in your knowledge of God" (Ephesians 1:17). And James wrote, "If you need wisdom—if you want to know what God wants you to do—ask him, and he will gladly tell you. He will not resent your asking" (James 1:5).

We must be open to the possibility that we are spiritually blind to our own faults or misinterpretations of life. We must not assume that we can see the truth—sometimes truth is obscured by ignorance, deception, or denial. Seeing the truth requires God's wisdom, which is available to all his children. All we need to do is recognize our need, open ourselves to God, ask him to give us his wisdom, and believe that he will. Then he will help us see the truth from his perspective.

■ **Key Two: See the Truth**
Day 2: Looking in the Mirror (James 1:21-25)

How many times do we look in the mirror each day? Most of us check up on our appearance quite frequently, and if we notice, for example, that we have something smeared around our mouth, we immediately wipe off our face and clear up the problem. In the same way, we need to routinely look at ourselves in a spiritual mirror, reflecting honestly on our spiritual condition as compared to God's Word. Then we need to make any necessary changes.

James says that God's Word is like a spiritual mirror. He said, "If you just listen and don't obey, it is like looking at your face in a mirror but doing nothing to improve your appearance. You see yourself, walk away, and forget what you look like. But if you keep looking steadily into God's perfect law—the law that sets you free—and if you do what it says and don't forget what you heard, then God will bless you for doing it" (James 1:23-25).

We need to regularly examine our lives by looking into God's Word. If we see that we have fallen short of something God requires, we need to take responsibility for it and take immediate action to correct it. Seeing the truth of our behavior is necessary for our spiritual renewal and transformation.

- ### Key Two: See the Truth
  Day 3: Temptation Is a Part of Life (1 Corinthians 10:12-13)

It is essential that we see the reality of temptation in our lives and stop denying its existence. Temptation is part of the human condition. If we think we're beyond its reach, we are not seeing the truth.

The Bible affirms that everyone experiences temptation: "Remember that the temptations that come into your life are no different from what others experience" (1 Corinthians 10:13). Not only is temptation all around us; it is within us as well. "Temptation comes from the lure of our own evil desires" (James 1:14). Even if we could rid ourselves of all external temptations, we would still have to live with the destructive desires hidden within us.

When we receive Christ as our Savior, God gives us a new nature. However, our human weaknesses are still with us—they will never completely go away in this life. That is why temptation will not magically disappear. When we acknowledge that we will always be susceptible to temptation, especially in our own personal areas of weakness, we are facing reality. Seeing this truth clearly help us to avoid falling under temptation's power and enables us to approach life with our eyes wide open to what lies ahead.

- **Key Two: See the Truth**
Day 4: Openness to God's Light (John 3:18-21)

Seeing the truth is dependent on our openness to God's light. God offers us all the light we need, but there may be some aspects of the truth we would rather not see, some areas of our lives we would rather not open to God's light. We may want to hide our areas of shame, areas of compromise that we know will look different under God's light, or areas where we hide the secret sins we aren't ready to give up. Darkness is great for hiding, but we need light to see the truth.

When talking about those who refused to trust him with their lives, Jesus said, "The light from heaven came into the world, but they loved the darkness more than the light, for their actions were evil. . . . They stay away from the light for fear their sins will be exposed and they will be punished" (John 3:19-20). Later, in one of his talks, Jesus said to the people, "I am the light of the world" (John 8:12).

We cannot fully see the truth unless we open our lives to God's light. But we can do this without fear because God has already offered to forgive us for anything we may be hiding in the shadows. Jesus Christ is the light of the world. His light dispels all the darkness in our souls.

- **Key Two: See the Truth**
Day 5: Growing Up in Truth (Ephesians 4:12-27)

In our relativistic world today, it is easy to ignore the truth about ourselves, especially when it makes us feel guilty. We can simply rationalize it away, claiming, "That may be true for you, but not for me." But if we to experience spiritual renewal, we must see the truth about ourselves. This includes growing in our knowledge of Jesus Christ and measuring our lives by his standard for truth.

The apostle Paul instructed the church that those who believed in

Christ were to function like a single body, with each member contributing in a special way to help God's people grow and mature in their understanding of the Lord (Ephesians 4:13). Once we reach maturity in our knowledge of Christ, "then we will no longer be like children, forever changing our minds about what we believe because someone has told us something different or because someone has cleverly lied to us and made the lie sound like the truth. Instead, we will hold to the truth in love, becoming more and more in every way like Christ" (Ephesians 4:14-15).

God wants us to grow spiritually, and that means growing to understand what is true. In the past we may have measured truth against whatever sounded right to us at the time. But now we must look to Jesus Christ, who is the truth. We must reevaluate our beliefs to conform them to his image.

■ **Key Three: Speak the Truth**
Day 1: The Plumb Line (Amos 7:7-8)

When we assess our moral character, we must base our measurements on truth. For if we measure ourselves against a faulty standard, we won't be able to see the truth and confess it to God.

In order to admonish the Israelites to admit their sin, the Lord used the analogy of a plumb line. "I will test my people with this plumb line. I will no longer ignore all their sins" (Amos 7:8). A plumb line is a length of string that has a weight tied to one end. When the string is held up with the weighted end hanging down, gravity ensures that the string is perfectly vertical. When held next to a building or structure, the plumb line provides something sure by which to check whether the building is correctly positioned. Unless a building is built in line with the plumb line, the structure will not stand as firm as it could.

The same holds true in the spiritual realm. God's Word is our spiritual plumb line. Just as we can't argue with the law of gravity, we can't change the spiritual laws revealed in the Bible. It is to our advantage to measure our lives by the plumb line of God's Word. When things don't measure up, it is important that we admit there is a problem and start rebuilding accordingly.

■ **Key Three: Speak the Truth**
Day 2: Unending Love (Hosea 11:8-11)

We may hesitate to honestly confess our sins and shortcomings out of fear. At one time or another, we may have tried to share our secrets with someone, only to find ourselves rejected because of what we said. Even though people may have let us down, God is not like that. Because of the sacrifice of Jesus Christ, there is nothing we could confess to God that would cause him to stop loving and accepting us.

Hosea was a prophet to the rebellious nation of Israel. God used Hosea's life to demonstrate his unconditional love for us. The Lord told Hosea to marry a prostitute. So Hosea married her, loved her, and devoted himself to her. Not surprisingly, she went back to her old ways, broke Hosea's heart, and brought shame on their family. She ended up falling into slavery. But God baffled Hosea by telling him, "Go and get your wife again. Bring her back to you and love her, even though she loves adultery. For the LORD still loves Israel even though the people have turned to other gods" (Hosea 3:1).

This illustrates God's love for us as well. We may ask, *How could God (or anyone) still love me?* But God asks, "How can I let you go? How can I destroy you like Admah and Zeboiim? My heart is torn within me, and my compassion overflows. . . . I am God and not a mere mortal. I am the Holy One living among you, and I will not come to destroy" (Hosea 11:8-9).

Like Hosea's unfaithful wife, we may have committed sins that seem unforgivable. Yet these verses give us hope: There is absolutely nothing we can do or admit that would cause God to stop loving us (see Romans 8:38-39). Knowing this, we should be encouraged to confess our sins to God, who offers us forgiveness and restoration.

■ **Key Three: Speak the Truth**
Day 3: Receiving Forgiveness (Acts 26:12-18)

Confessing our sins to God and to others allows us to humble ourselves and to share our weaknesses. We should confess our sins and encourage others to do likewise. In doing so, we can help others live in the light and speak the truth before God.

Jesus gave the apostle Paul, this mission: "I have appeared to you to appoint you as my servant and my witness. . . . Yes, I am going to send you to the Gentiles, to open their eyes so they may turn from darkness to light, and from the power of Satan to God. Then they will receive forgiveness for their sins and be given a place among God's people, who are set apart by faith in me" (Acts 26:16-18).

Once we are honest before God and admit our wrongs, we begin to dispel the darkness in our lives. God wants us to live in the light, to receive immediate forgiveness based on the finished work of Jesus Christ. A restored relationship with God awaits us right now if we will confess our sins and receive his forgiveness.

■ **Key Three: Speak the Truth**
Day 4: Choosing Trustworthy Friends (Judges 16:1-31)

Once we have committed ourselves to confessing our faults and weaknesses to others, it is extremely important for us to keep company with trustworthy people—godly people we can entrust with our confidences. Otherwise, we will find it impossible to speak the truth and may even find ourselves lying because we can't trust our friends.

Samson was one of Israel's judges. As a child, he had been dedicated to God, and God had gifted him with supernatural strength. But Samson had a lifelong weakness—his desire for women. Samson was especially blinded to the dangers he faced in his relationship with Delilah. Samson's enemies paid Delilah to discover the secret of his strength. Three times she begged him to let her in on his secret, and each time she tried to use this information to hand him over to his enemies. All three times, Samson lied to her and was able to escape, but each time he got closer to telling her the truth. In the end, Samson revealed his secret, was taken captive, and died a slave in enemy hands (Judges 14–16).

Samson's real problem can be found in his unholy passions, which caused him to be drawn into the web of his treacherous enemies. His disobedience to God caused him to gradually inch his way toward destruction and a violent death.

We can protect ourselves from falling into the same trap by obeying God and developing relationships with those who love us and are devoted to God's truth. Trustworthy confidants can be relied upon to hear us speak about both our strengths and our weaknesses.

■ Key Three: Speak the Truth
Day 5: Honestly Admitting Our Needs (Luke 11:5-13)

Part of speaking the truth involves admitting that we have needs. We must rid ourselves of pride and self-sufficiency, which forbid us to confess that we are vulnerable or dependent on others. But confessing our needs can be just as important as confessing our sins and shortcomings.

In order to show that God wants us to ask him for what we need, Jesus urged his followers, "Keep on asking, and you will be given what you ask for. Keep on looking, and you will find. Keep on knocking, and the door will be opened. For everyone who asks, receives. Everyone who seeks, finds. And the door is opened to everyone who knocks" (Luke 11:9-10). Jesus also said, "You parents—if your children ask for a loaf of bread, do you give them a stone instead? Or if they ask for a fish, do you give them a snake? Of course not! If you sinful people know how to give good gifts to your children, how much more will your heavenly Father give good gifts to those who ask him" (Matthew 7:9-11).

God wants to give us good things. But we must humbly admit that we have needs, and we must even be willing, if God directs us to do so, to ask others for help. And we can't ask God for help just once and be done with it. We must be persistent and ask repeatedly, confessing our needs to him as they arise. We can be assured that our loving heavenly Father will respond lovingly—perhaps through the generosity of others.

■ **Key Four: Accept Responsibility**
Day 1: Obeying the Holy Spirit (Galatians 5:16-23)

As we take responsibility for our lives, we must also take responsibility to obey the Holy Spirit's instructions. Then, as we continue the process of spiritual renewal, God's Spirit will begin to produce fruit in our lives.

The apostle Paul explained it in this way:

> So I advise you to live according to your new life in the Holy Spirit. Then you won't be doing what your sinful nature craves. The old sinful nature loves to do evil, which is just opposite from what the Holy Spirit wants. And the Spirit gives us desires that are opposite from what the sinful nature desires. These two forces are constantly fighting each other, and your choices are never free from this conflict. . . . But when the Holy Spirit controls our lives, he will produce this kind of fruit in us: love, joy, peace, patience, kindness, goodness, faithfulness, gentleness, and self-control. (Galatians 5:16-17, 22-23)

Fruit doesn't instantly appear on trees. As trees grow and seasons pass, fruit slowly develops. In a similar way, as we continue to accept our responsibility to obey the Holy Spirit, good spiritual fruit will begin to appear in our lives. Our primary responsibility is to stay connected to God. It is the Holy Spirit's responsibility to produce good fruit in us.

- **Key Four: Accept Responsibility**
  Day 2: Responsible to Love (1 Corinthians 13:1-7)

True love is not something we "fall into" or "fall out of." The kind of love God tells us to show for others is not an event we simply wait for, nor is it an experience that happens to us. Love is what God commands us to do. Love is a responsibility. And we cannot truly love as God commands apart from a relationship with God, who is love.

If we do not have love, nothing else matters (see 1 Corinthians 13:1-4). Love is a fruit of the Holy Spirit, produced in our lives as we yield ourselves to God. The Bible defines it this way: "Love is patient and kind. Love is not jealous or boastful or proud or rude. Love does not demand its own way. Love is not irritable, and it keeps no record of when it has been wronged. It is never glad about injustice but rejoices whenever the truth wins out. Love never gives up, never loses faith, is always hopeful, and endures through every circumstance" (1 Corinthians 13:4-7).

This passage is a description of how God loves us. As we begin to absorb his love, we will find ourselves reaching out to love others in this same way. No one loves perfectly, but we must not give up on loving. We cannot expect to be good at loving right away; we can be patient as God's love grows within us. We can accept the responsibility to love others and stop waiting for them to love us. When we choose to act in loving ways, the emotions will follow. We will find that love grows in our lives as we accept our responsibility to love and ask God to let his love flow through us.

- **Key Four: Accept Responsibility**
  Day 3: Making the Best of a Bad Situation (1 Samuel 25:18-39)

There will be times when those close to us make wrong choices or act irresponsibly, creating a bad situation that threatens our well-being or spiritual growth. We are not responsible for their actions or the bad situation they create. However, we are responsible to protect ourselves and make the best of a bad situation.

Abigail is a good example of someone who took responsibility to make the best of a bad situation. Her husband, Nabal (meaning "fool"), was "mean and dishonest in all his dealings" (1 Samuel 25:3). Before David became king, Nabal insulted his troops to the point that David and his men were on their way to kill him and anyone who got in their way. Through some fast thinking and some even faster talking, however, Abigail protected her family. She convinced David not to take vengeance into his own hands. A few weeks later Nabal was dead of natural, or perhaps supernatural, causes, and Abigail became David's wife.

We cannot always change other people; that is not our responsibility. But even when we can't change them, we can still make good choices in the midst of bad situations. We are not responsible for changing the character flaws of the people who affect our lives. We *are* responsible for protecting ourselves, as best we can, from the effects of their irresponsible behavior.

■ Key Four: Accept Responsibility
Day 4: Unable to Remove Sinfulness (Romans 6:5-11)

We must take responsibility for our lives and to stop trying to pass the blame for our sins onto others. But, believe it or not, we are not responsible for transforming our sinful nature. Most of us have made numerous attempts at self-improvement. Perhaps we have consciously tried to improve our attitudes, our education, our appearance, or our habits, and that's good. We probably have even had success in self-improvement on some level. However, when it comes to our struggles with our sinful nature, chances are we have only experienced deep frustration when we tried to change.

There is a reason for our frustration when we try to transform our sinful nature by our own power: Our sinful nature can only be transformed by God. The Bible tells us that our sinful nature must be put to death, as Jesus was, if we are to find hope for new life. The apostle Paul wrote, "Our old sinful selves were crucified with Christ so that sin might lose its power in our lives. We are no longer slaves to sin" (Romans 6:6). And again, "Those who belong to Christ Jesus have nailed the passions and desires of their sinful nature to his cross and crucified them there" (Galatians 5:24).

There is no quick fix for our sinful nature, and we are not responsible to improve it. We are only responsible to allow God to put our old nature to death daily. When we stop trying to improve that part of us that cannot be improved, God can crucify our old nature and resurrect a new life in its place. That is true spiritual renewal.

- ### Key Four: Accept Responsibility
  Day 5: Being Responsible to Do What We Can Do (Judges 5:1-12)

There are times when others fail to fulfill their responsibilities. When this happens, we may suffer from their lack of discipline. We may feel frustrated and angry, but that should not keep us from doing our part. Even when others refuse to do their part, we must accept responsibility to do what we can do.

The time of the judges was a time of confusion for Israel. The people did what was right in their own eyes instead of obeying God's law. They were oppressed by tyrants, one of whom was Sisera, who "ruthlessly oppressed the Israelites for twenty years" (Judges 4:3). At this time God chose Deborah to be a judge. Her job was to settle the disputes of the people. One day Deborah summoned a man named Barak and told him that God would use him to defeat the army of Sisera. Barak said, "I will go, but only if you go with me!" (Judges 4:8). So Deborah agreed to go along, but she added, "You will receive no honor. For the LORD's victory over Sisera will be at the hands of a woman" (Judges 4:9). Barak lacked the faith to take on the responsibilities God had given him. In the end, Sisera did die at the hands of a woman. In the victory song, Deborah was honored. They sang, "There were few people left in the villages of Israel—until Deborah arose as a mother for Israel" (Judges 5:7).

Like Deborah, when others don't fulfill their rightful duties and roles, we still must find a way to do what is right. We cannot blame others for our own behavior and lack of spiritual growth.

■ Key Five: Grieve, Forgive, and Let Go

Day 1: Help for the Brokenhearted (Lamentations 3:1-26)

Even though we are seeking God and pursuing spiritual renewal, we are not exempt from suffering. We may encounter tragedy, or we may suffer by watching loved ones bear the consequences of their own resistance to God. Whenever our hearts are breaking, we should release our grief and sorrow to God, who can mend our broken hearts.

Jeremiah watched as his beloved nation was taken captive, ravished, and almost completely destroyed because of its own refusal to surrender to God. It's no wonder Jeremiah is known as the weeping prophet. Lamentations is a record of Jeremiah's lament over the shameful fate of God's people. He cried:

> My splendor is gone! Everything I had hoped for from the LORD is lost! The thought of my suffering and homelessness is bitter beyond words. I will never forget this awful time, as I grieve over my loss. Yet I still dare to hope when I remember this: The unfailing love of the LORD never ends! By his mercies we have been kept from complete destruction. Great is his faithfulness; his mercies begin afresh each day. . . . The LORD is wonderfully good to those who wait for him and seek him. (Lamentations 3:18-25)

Releasing our lives to God means forgiving those who have contributed to our pain and giving God our pain and suffering. In our times of grief and shame, we can hope for the time when God will overcome the problems we face. God is strong enough to lift our burdens and loving enough to mend our broken hearts. We must remind ourselves of God's love for us.

■ **Key Five: Grieve, Forgive, and Let Go**
Day 2: Relinquishing the Debts Owed Us (Matthew 18:23-35)

We tend to keep a running list of the wrongs that have been done against us and an accounting of what we think others owe us for what they have done. We may feel they owe us an apology, a sum of money, or perhaps their lives. In our minds, every time we are hurt, the ones who hurt us incur a moral debt. Relinquishing these accounts to God and forgiving the debts we feel others owe us is essential to our spiritual growth.

Jesus told a story: "A king . . . decided to bring his accounts up to date. . . . In the process, one of his debtors was brought in who owed him millions of dollars" (Matthew 18:23-24). The man begged for forgiveness. "Then the king was filled with pity for him, and he released him and forgave his debt. But when the man left the king, he went to a fellow servant who owed him a few thousand dollars. He grabbed him by the throat and demanded instant payment" (Matthew 18:27-28). This was reported to the king. "Then the king called in the man he had forgiven and said, 'You evil servant! I forgave you that tremendous debt because you pleaded with me. Shouldn't you have mercy on your fellow servant, just as I had mercy on you?' Then the angry king sent the man to prison until he had paid every penny. That's what my heavenly Father will do to you if you refuse to forgive your brothers and sisters in your heart" (Matthew 18:32-35).

When we look at the enormous moral debt God has forgiven us in Christ, we should be compelled to forgive others. This also frees us from the torture of festering resentment. We can't change what others have done to us, but we can write off their debts by handing the accounting process over to God.

■ **Key Five: Grieve, Forgive, and Let Go**
Day 3: Releasing Our Sorrow Makes Way for Joy (Nehemiah 8:7-10)

In order to release the past into God's hands, we must fully encounter our grief, and we must be willing to forgive ourselves and others for the pain that has occurred.

Many of the Jewish exiles who returned to Jerusalem after captivity in Babylon had forgotten the laws of God. During the Exile, they hadn't been taught his laws, so, naturally, they hadn't practiced them either. After rebuilding the city wall and the Temple, the priests gathered the people together to read the Book of the Law. The people were overwhelmed with grief and began sobbing because their lives in no way measured up. But the priests said to them:

> Don't weep on such a day as this! For today is a sacred day before the LORD your God. . . . Go and celebrate with a feast of choice foods and sweet drinks, and share gifts of food with people who have nothing prepared. This is a sacred day before our Lord. Don't be dejected and sad, for the joy of the LORD is your strength! (Nehemiah 8:9-10)

That day marked the beginning of the Festival of Shelters, which celebrated their escape from bondage in Egypt and God's care for them while they wandered in the wilderness.

Although the process of releasing the past may require grief, as well as forgiveness, we have been given the "joy of the LORD" as our strength. This joy comes from recognizing, even celebrating, God's ability to set us free from the past and, in doing so, to prepare us a new way of life.

■ **Key Five: Grieve, Forgive, and Let Go**
Day 4: Sorrow Can Be Good For Us (2 Corinthians 7:8-11)

Sometimes forgiving others or ourselves involves pain. When we confront people regarding betrayal, abandonment, abuse, deception, or other offenses, we are likely to be faced with deep sorrow. Even true forgiveness does not always completely remove the pain we feel. We need to accept this kind of pain as part of the consequences of sin and learn to freely express it to God. He can use the pain associated with wrongdoing and bring about good in our lives.

Not all sorrow is bad for us. The apostle Paul had written a letter to the Corinthians and made them very sad because he confronted them about something that they were doing wrong. At first he was

221

sorry that he had hurt them, but later he said, "Now I am glad I sent it, not because it hurt you, but because the pain caused you to have remorse and change your ways. It was the kind of sorrow God wants his people to have, so you were not harmed by us in any way. For God can use sorrow in our lives to help us turn away from sin and seek salvation. We will never regret that kind of sorrow" (2 Corinthians 7:9-11).

The grief Paul described was good, for it came from honest self-evaluation, not morbid self-condemnation. We can learn to accept our sorrow for sin as a positive part of our spiritual growth. Whenever we encounter sorrow, we should ask God to use it to help us redirect the course of our lives.

■ Key Five: Grieve, Forgive, and Let Go
Day 5: Forgiving Ourselves (John 21:14-25)

For most of the sins we commit, we are grateful and eager to accept God's forgiveness. But sometimes we are so shocked at our own behavior, so ashamed of the way we behaved, so heartbroken over how we have hurt others that we find it hard to believe that God could really forgive us. Yet God *is* willing to forgive us—and even more, he desires to restore us, to redirect our course, and to redeem our lives for his service. But this restoration cannot begin until we receive God's forgiveness and forgive ourselves.

Peter had once sworn his love for Jesus. He boasted that if everyone else abandoned Jesus, he would not; he pledged even to die with Jesus if necessary. Yet that same night after Jesus was arrested, Peter sheepishly protected himself by denying that he even knew Jesus. Jesus wasn't surprised; he had already told Peter that Peter would deny him three times before the night was out. Jesus was ready to forgive Peter before he even committed the sins. But Peter had a hard time forgiving himself. After Jesus rose from the dead, he had this conversation with Peter.

> Jesus said to Simon Peter, "Simon son of John, do you love me more than these?" "Yes, Lord," Peter replied, "You know I love you." . . . [A third time Jesus] asked him, "Simon son of John, do you love me?" Peter was grieved that Jesus asked the ques-

tion a third time. He said, "Lord, you know everything. You know I love you." (John 21:15-17)

Peter denied Jesus three times, and Jesus gave Peter the chance to reaffirm his love three times. Jesus reached out to Peter when Peter didn't feel worthy to reach out to him. When we are disheartened by our own sinfulness, it is difficult to receive God's forgiveness. But God is reaching out to forgive us of all our sins. Once we confess our sins, we need to let go of them and realize that Jesus paid for each and every one. Then we can accept God's forgiveness and get on with our lives. At times like these, it also helps to reaffirm our love for God.

■ **Key Six: Transform Your Life**
Day 1: Faith to Build a New Life (1 Chronicles 28:1-21)

Our past sometimes gets in the way of our vision for the future. If we allow ourselves to dwell on the areas in which we have failed or on the losses and disappointments that have hurt us, we may find it difficult to look forward to the future God has for us.

King David dreamed of building a magnificent temple. In commissioning his son Solomon to do the work he said, "Be strong and courageous, and do the work. Don't be afraid or discouraged by the size of the task, for the LORD God, my God, is with you. He will not fail you or forsake you" (1 Chronicles 28:20). Many years later the apostle Paul said, "We who believe are carefully joined together, becoming a holy temple for the Lord" (Ephesians 2:21).

Just as David dreamed of building a magnificent temple, we can dare to dream of building a magnificent new life. God has the blueprint already drawn up; all we have to do is follow it by faith. We may be afraid that we will start and fail, but we need only to "be strong and courageous, and do the work." We need not be frightened by the size of the task, for "God, who began the good work within you, will continue his work until it is finally finished on that day when Christ Jesus comes back again" (Philippians 1:6).

■ **Key Six: Transform Your Life**
Day 2: From the Past to the Future

God wants to move us out of our sinful past and into a better future. As we cooperate with God's process of redeeming our past, we need to honestly evaluate our lives so that we can redirect our course according to God's design.

Jesus said, "You will know the truth, and the truth will set you free" (John 8:32). The path to freedom always leads through the truth, even the truth about our past. Paul examined his past, making an honest review of his earthly accomplishments, his wrongs, his mistakes, his gains, and his losses. It was from this broad perspective that he wrote: "I don't mean to say that I have already achieved these things or that I have already reached perfection! But I keep working toward that day when I will finally be all that Christ Jesus saved me for and wants me to be" (Philippians 3:12).

Freedom from the past also involves facing up to the times when others have harmed us and turning them over to God. The apostle Paul once wrote to young Timothy: "Alexander the coppersmith has done me much harm, but the Lord will judge him for what he has done" (2 Timothy 4:14). Paul states the truth about someone who had hurt him but leaves the matter in God's hands.

When we hand over our past to God with the prayer that he work it out for the best according to his will, we can finally let go of it. Then we can redirect our course toward a brighter future and help others to do the same through the lessons we have learned.

■ Key Six: Transform Your Life
Day 3: Fulfilling Our Mission (Isaiah 61:1-3)

A life that has been set free from sin is a beautiful sight. When we turn from our sins and live as God has planned for us, we testify to the glory of God and give others hope that he can change their lives. We may know from experience the suffering, affliction, and brokenness that come from going our own way. We may know what it is like to be enslaved to our passions. Yet we also know that there is more to life than bondage. There is healing and freedom; there is beauty and joy; there is love and mercy. And we have the wonderful privilege of proclaiming this Good News to those around us.

Jesus was commissioned with this same task—to bring Good News to those who are broken. He began his ministry by quoting these verses from Isaiah: "The Spirit of the Sovereign LORD is upon me, because the LORD has appointed me to bring good news to the poor. He has sent me to comfort the brokenhearted and to announce that captives will be released and prisoners will be freed. He has sent me to tell those who mourn that the time of the LORD's favor has come" (Isaiah 61:1-2).

We were once on our way to destruction, but God redirected us toward his Way—Jesus Christ. When we surrendered our lives to Jesus, we started on the path to heaven. Now we are called to bring this Good News to others, urging them to turn from their own way and follow the Lord.

■ **Key Six: Transform Your Life**
Day 4: Faith to Enter the Promised Land (Joshua 1:1-9)

Detours and delays, often the results of our fears and our unfaithfulness, frequently hinder us in our journey toward spiritual growth. Yet God has still promised to bring a joyous outcome to our difficult journey—to lead us from the dry, arid wilderness of our lives into a fruitful Promised Land. So why do we allow our doubts and insecurities to slow our spiritual progress?

God led the nation of Israel out of bondage in Egypt, through the wilderness, to the edge of the Promised Land. But as they stood on the border, looking into the fruitful and prosperous land of Canaan, the Israelites lacked the faith and courage to go in. As a result, they wandered for forty years in the wilderness, and only their descendants (with the exception of Joshua and Caleb) were allowed to enter the Promised Land. Just before they entered the land, the Lord told them, "Be strong and courageous! Do not be afraid or discouraged. For the LORD your God is with you wherever you go" (Joshua 1:9).

Like the Israelites, we have received promises of blessing from the Lord. The Lord revealed his desires for his people when he asserted, "'For I know the plans I have for you. . . . They are plans for good and not for disaster, to give you a future and a hope" (Jeremiah 29:11). No matter how long we have been lost in the wilderness, and no matter how hopeless the future may yet seem, God can transform our years of wandering into a purposeful journey and lead us into the land he has promised us.

■ **Key Six: Transform Your Life**
Day 5: Sharing God's Message (Acts 8:26-40)

When God begins to transform our lives, we may become so excited that we want to rush right out and tell everyone about the exciting changes he is making. God will lead us to people with whom we can share the Good News. We can make the most of these opportunities by paying attention to the way God is leading and by communicating the message effectively.

The evangelist Philip was led to meet an influential traveler who had gone to Jerusalem to worship and was returning to his native land. When Philip came upon him he was "reading aloud from the book of the prophet Isaiah. The Holy Spirit said to Philip, 'Go over and walk along beside the carriage.' Philip ran over and heard the man reading from the prophet Isaiah; so he asked, 'Do you understand what you are reading?' The man replied, 'How can I, when there is no one to instruct me?' . . . So Philip began with this same Scripture and then used many others to tell him the Good News about Jesus" (Acts 8:28-31, 35).

The way Philip communicated the Good News is a model for us to follow. He sensitively allowed God to lead him to someone who was ready to receive the Good News. Then Philip listened carefully to the man's needs and interests and showed him how Christ could fulfill them. The man gladly received the message, was baptized immediately, and went home a changed man. Whether we are zealous or shy, following this model can help us communicate our message in a way that people can receive and understand. In this way, God will use us to transform their lives as well as our own.

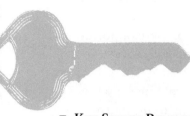

■ Key Seven: Preserve Spiritual Gains
Day 1: Perseverance throughout Life (2 Timothy 2:1-8)

Spiritual renewal and growth are a lifelong process. There will be times when we grow weary, times when we want to throw in the towel. We will experience pain, fear, and a host of other emotions. We will win some battles but lose others. We may get discouraged at times when we can't see any progress, even though we have been working hard. But if we persevere through it all, we will preserve our spiritual gains.

The apostle Paul used three illustrations to teach about perseverance. He wrote to Timothy:

> "Endure suffering along with me, as a good soldier of Christ Jesus. And as Christ's soldier, do not let yourself become tied up in the affairs of this life, for then you cannot satisfy the one who has enlisted you in his army. Follow the Lord's rules for doing his work, just as an athlete either follows the rules or is disqualified and wins no prize. Hardworking farmers are the first to enjoy the fruit of their labor" (2 Timothy 2:3-6).

Like soldiers, we are in a war that we can win only if we fight to the end. Like athletes running a marathon, we must follow God all the way to the finish line. Like farmers, we must do our work in every season and then wait patiently to reap the benefits of our labor. If we stop before reaching our goal, we may lose the spiritual gains and everything else for which we have fought, trained, and worked hard.

- **Key Seven: Preserve Spiritual Gains**
Day 2: Gently and Humbly Correcting Each Other (John 15:5-15)

Sometimes, in our network of support and accountability, we will need to correct others regarding sin; sometimes they will need to correct us regarding our sin. When touching on such deep and sensitive issues, it is important to speak in the language of love, not condemnation. While this is a delicate matter, our willingness to correct others and to be corrected in accordance with God's Word will help preserve spiritual gains.

The Bible tells us that "if another Christian is overcome by some sin, you who are godly should gently and humbly help that person back onto the right path. And be careful not to fall into the same temptation yourself. Share each other's troubles and problems, and in this way obey the law of Christ" (Galatians 6:1-2). This command of Paul's is the same as the one Jesus taught his disciples: "So now I am giving you a new commandment: Love each other. Just as I have loved you, you should love each other" (John 13:34). Jesus reiterated this instruction later, saying, "I command you to love each other in the same way that I love you. And here is how to measure it—the greatest love is shown when people lay down their lives for their friends" (John 15:12-13).

We must try to love others as our Savior has loved us. Love goes beyond mere words. Sometimes it is spoken in silence when we don't condemn someone who comes to us looking for help. Love doesn't just speak words of righteousness—it helps carry the weight of others' burdens. Other times love does require that we compassionately confront others with the truth of their sin. We can be part of a support network to help carry our friends, just as they help us preserve spiritual gains by carrying us as well.

- **Key Seven: Preserve Spiritual Gains**
Day 3: A Day of Rest (Exodus 31:12-13)

Seeking to preserve our spiritual gains requires a balanced life. We need to get enough rest, including the discipline of taking one day of rest each week. If we allow ourselves to get overtired, we will be less able to cope with the demands of life. And it will be harder for us to maintain our spiritual gains.

The Bible recognizes the importance of rest for people, for farmland, and for animals. Even God himself rested on the seventh day of creation (Genesis 2:2-3). Weekly rest was included as one of the Ten Commandments. God declared:

> Six days a week are set apart for your daily duties and regular work, but the seventh day is a day of rest dedicated to the LORD your God. On that day no one in your household may do any kind of work. . . . For in six days the LORD made the heavens, the earth, the sea, and everything in them; then he rested on the seventh day. That is why the LORD blessed the Sabbath day and set it apart as holy. (Exodus 20:9-11)

The Lord further instructed the Israelites, "Keep my Sabbath day, for the Sabbath is a sign of the covenant between me and you forever. It helps you to remember that I am the LORD, who makes you holy" (Exodus 31:12-13).

God wants us to have the rest we need for a balanced life. A weekly Sabbath also reminds us that we follow the Lord. This should be a time to relax from our regular duties and reflect on God's promises and remember that it is God who sustains us.

■ **Key Seven: Preserve Spiritual Gains**
Day 4: Waiting for the Lord to Renew Us (Isaiah 40:28-31)

It is a continual challenge to wait patiently on the Lord, no matter how far we have progressed in our spiritual growth. In order to preserve our spiritual gains, we must constantly remember to practice the *first* key to renewal: seeking God and surrendering to him.

The prophet Isaiah gave us this promise: "Those who wait on the LORD will find new strength. They will fly high on wings like eagles. They will run and not grow weary. They will walk and not faint" (Isaiah 40:31). Jeremiah said, "The LORD is wonderfully good to those who wait for him and seek him. So it is good to wait quietly for salvation from the LORD" (Lamentations 3:25-26).

The Lord will reward us for waiting upon him. We can remain

calm when it appears that nothing is happening in our spiritual lives. As we learn to respond to life in new ways, the winds of adversity will lift us up, like wind beneath the wings of an eagle, instead of knocking us down. As we develop a patient faith in God, we will be able to endure to the end of the race—and win. As we seek God and wait on him to complete his work in our lives, we will be continually renewed.

■ Key Seven: Preserve Spiritual Gains
Day 5: At the Cross (Matthew 26:36-39)

Our spiritual journey is not always an easy one. As we travel the long, difficult road that God is calling us to walk, we must bear a cross. That cross represents our death to our sinful desires and ways of life. But the way of the cross always leads to a resurrection and new life. When we think about the cross we must bear, we need to surrender to God so that we won't give up or stumble beneath the weight.

As God leads us to do his will instead of our own, we may wish there were some other way. We may feel fear, a lack of confidence, deep anguish, and a host of other emotions that threaten to stop us in our tracks. Regardless of our feelings, we must not let them cause us to turn away from the path God sets before us.

Jesus understands our fears and our struggle to persevere. He had similar emotions the night he was arrested. His friends—Peter, James, and John—were nearby, but when he needed them they were asleep. He told them, "My soul is crushed with grief to the point of death" (Matthew 26:38). As he realized the enormity of the pain he would face, he wondered if there were some other way. He struggled and prayed the same basic prayer three times, "My Father! If it is possible, let this cup of suffering be taken away from me. Yet I want your will, not mine" (Matthew 26:39). As we can see from the end of his prayer, however, Jesus found the grace to accept God's plan.

We may be overwhelmed as we consider the cross we will have to bear on the way to a new life. But during such times of struggle, we can go to Jesus for encouragement and express our deepest emotions. As we cry out for help, we can be confident that we will be given the strength we need to do God's will rather than our own. Our perseverance at such times and our renewed commitment to surrender our lives to God will be richly rewarded.